KT-592-260

READING POETRY
A Contextual Introduction

John Williams
Lecturer in English, Thames Polytechnic

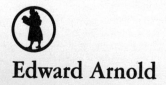

Edward Arnold

821.009

LIVERPOOL POLYTECHNIC
C.F. MOTT CAMPUS
LIBRARY
267261

© John Williams 1985

First published in Great Britain 1985 by
Edward Arnold (Publishers) Ltd, 41 Bedford Square,
London WC1B 3DQ

Edward Arnold (Australia) Pty Ltd,
80 Waverley Road, Caulfield East, Victoria 3145, Australia

British Library Cataloguing in Publication Data

Williams, John
    Reading poetry: a contextual introduction.
    1. English poetry——History and criticism
    I. Title
    821'.009   PR502

ISBN 0-7131-6455-7

All rights reserved. No part of this publication may be reproduced,
stored in a retrieval system, or transmitted in any form or by any
means, electronic, photocopying, recording, or otherwise, without the
prior permission of Edward Arnold (Publishers) Ltd.

Text set in 10/11 pt Garamond Compugraphic
by Colset Private Ltd, Singapore
Printed and bound by Richard Clay (The Chaucer Press) Ltd,
Bungay, Suffolk.

CONTENTS

For Anne and Mark

NOTES ON TEXTS AND REFERENCES

Details of quoted material are given in the text. The following abbreviations and references have been used to identify editions:

Absalom and Achitophel	*The Poems and Fables of John Dryden*, ed. James Kinsley (London, Oxford University Press, 1962).
AP	*American Poetry*, ed. Donald Hall (London, Faber and Faber, 1969).
BP	*British Poetry Since 1945*, ed. Edward Lucie-Smith (London, Penguin, 1970).
EEP	*The Earliest English Poems*, ed. Michael Alexander (London, Penguin, 1966).
GMH	*Gerard Manley Hopkins*, ed. W.H. Gardner (London, Penguin, 1970).
Idylls of the King	*Idylls of the King*, ed. J.M. Gray (London, Penguin, 1983).
PAP	*The Poems of Alexander Pope*, ed. John Butt (London, Methuen, 1978).
PBAV	*The Penguin Book of American Verse*, (revised edition) ed. Geoffrey Moore (London, Penguin, 1983).
PBEV	*The Penguin Book of Elizabethan Verse*, ed. Edward Lucie-Smith (London, Penguin, 1965).
PBRV	*The Penguin Book of English Romantic Verse*, ed. David Wright (London, Penguin, 1968).
PFD	*Poems of Faith and Doubt*, ed. R.L. Brett (London, Edward Arnold, 1965).
PJM	*The Poems of John Milton*, ed. John Carey and Alastair Fowler (London, Longman, 1968).

SP   *Silver Poets of the Sixteenth Century*, ed.
                      Gerald Bullet (London, Dent, 1978).

The Faerie   *The Faerie Queene*, ed. Thomas P. Roche
Queene   (London, Penguin, 1978).

The First   *John Donne, Complete English Poems*, ed.
Anniversarie   Albert James Smith (London, Penguin, 1982).

The Waste Land   T.S. Eliot, *Collected Poems 1909–1962*
                      (London, Faber and Faber, 1963).

TLA   *The Late Augustans*, ed. Donald Davie
                      (London, Heinemann, 1958).

TMP   *The Metaphysical Poets*, ed. Helen Gardner
                      (London, Penguin, 1972).

TNP   *The New Poetry*, A. Alvarez (London,
                      Penguin, 1970).

WPW   *Wordsworth, Poetical Works*, ed. Thomas
                      Hutchinson, revised by Ernest de Selincourt
                      (London, Oxford University Press, 1969).

PREFACE

This book explores just one approach among many to the problem of how we 'read' poetry. It combines a sense of a poem's context with the ability to analyse it technically, but the emphasis lies ultimately with context as the most helpful guide to a poem's meaning.

By technical analysis, I mean the study of a poem's form in terms of metre, rhyme scheme (if it has one), and the detailed description of the way words and phrases have been chosen. Such things have a crucial part to play in the reading of any poem, and they are referred to extensively in this book.

Seeking out a poem's context requires us to consider the circumstances in which it was written. The kind of context investigated here is one which seeks to avoid too great an emphasis on immediate circumstances, and looks instead to a consideration of what was expected of poetry in any given period, and at the way the poet saw his function in relation to those expectations. The contextual approach retains a sense of the poem as belonging among other poems; as such a poet's work will bear the marks of certain inherited assumptions (often partly expressed through the poet's choice of style) while the poem will at the same time exist as an original statement, the property of the poet.

Using an analysis of technique as our primary means of reading a poem can effectively isolate that poem from all other poems. On occasion this may be no bad thing; but there remains, however, the disconcerting fact that poetry as a whole assumes a bewildering variety of forms. The mastery of a technical approach relevant to a sixteenth-century sonnet, for example, may well seem to get us nowhere with a twentieth-century specimen of 'concrete' poetry. This is not to say, of course, that there is not a technical means of analysing concrete poetry; but the difference between the two poems may consequently appear so extreme as to call in question the right of both to claim that they are 'poetry'.

If we work with context in mind, we will necessarily think in comparative terms, and a sense of the range of poetic expression may well positively help our reading.

It is to the question of variety of forms that we initially turn in Chapter 1, before comparing aspects of poetic composition in different historical periods. Some attempt at least must be made to consider a definition of what we read as 'poetry'. My point here will be that, different as some poems are stylistically, a common approach to the reading of poetry remains possible. In the chapters which follow, I hope to be able to illustrate this in practical terms through the analysis of poems and extracts from poems which accompanies the theoretical discussion of context.

Acknowledgements

I am indebted to my publishers for the patient help I received in the preparation of the text. The faults that remain are, however, unfortunately my own.

The publishers would like to thank the following for permission to include copyright poems: Carcanet Press Limited for extracts from Edwin Morgan, 'Pomander' and 'The Domain of Arnheim'; Curtis Brown for John Wain, 'The New Sun'; Faber and Faber publishers for extracts from Thom Gunn, 'A Mirror for Poets' from *Fighting Terms*, Ted Hughes, 'Hawk Roosting' from *Lupercal* and W. H. Auden, 'Embassy' from *Collected Poems*; Philip Hobsbaum for his poem 'A Secret Sharer'; Macmillan Publishing Co. Inc. for Hugh MacDiarmid, 'Glasgow 1960' from *Collected Poems*; New Directions Publishing Corporation for William Carlos Williams, 'Spring and All' from *Collected Earlier Poems*, copyright 1938 by New Directions Publishing Corporation and reprinted by permission; Oxford University Press for Charles Tomlinson, 'The Churchyard Wall' from *Selected Poems 1951-1974* © Charles Tomlinson 1978; and Deborah Rogers Ltd for Edward Lucie-Smith, 'The Bruise'.

1
WHAT IS A POEM?

Where's the poet? Show him, show him,
Muses nine, that I may know him!
'Tis the man who with a man
   Is an equal, be he king,
Or poorest of the beggar-clan. . .

           (Keats, *Where's the poet?* 1818)

The two passages of poetry I have chosen to discuss in some detail
in this chapter appear to be so different in just about every
respect, that the one descriptive term 'poetry' hardly seems ade-
quate to describe them both. There would be every justification
for the reader to assume that they have to be read in quite different ways. However, in discussing their characteristics, their
obvious differences, their less obvious similarities, we shall see if it
is possible to begin to answer the question: what is a poem? In so
doing we shall learn more about where to begin when we want to
know how to read a poem, and what we should be looking for.

    The following passage is the first verse from a poem by
Tennyson (1809–92), *Sir Galahad*:

My good blade carves the casques of men,	1
My tough lance thrusteth sure,	2
My strength is as the strength of ten,	3
Because my heart is pure.	4
The shattering trumpet thrilleth high,	5
The hard brands shiver on the steel,	6
The splinter'd spear-shafts crack and fly,	7
The horse and rider reel:	8
They reel, they roll in clanging lists,	9
And when the tide of combat stands,	10
Perfume and flowers fall in showers,	11
That lightly rain from ladies' hands.	12

My reason for beginning with this is that – whether we like the
piece or not – there is likely to be general agreement that it is
poetry, and it ought to be fairly easy to explain why we feel confident that it is so.

In the first place, the words are arranged in a series of specially ordered lines. Just seeing the *shape* of the verse on the page before we even begin to read the words, therefore, gives the impression of a carefully managed construction, an orderly arrangement of words. It looks the way poetry is generally expected to look. When we see the whole poem, which consists of seven such verses, our sense of structure and order is confirmed.

Beginning then to read, we note further evidence of the writer's management of words; very soon a regular rhyming pattern is evident, and that in conjunction with the line structure soon gives us a sense of rhythm. There are four heavy stresses in the first and third lines, three in the second and fourth. Above all we are conscious of Tennyson's control and manipulation of language. He uses not only vividly descriptive words, but actually reproduces something approaching the appropriate sound by the careful juxtaposition of consonants. Line seven is a good example of this 'alliteration': 'The *s*plinter'd *s*pear-*s*hafts crack and fly'. In line 11, to emphasize a softer, literally feminine touch, the gentler sound of the letter 'f' is used: 'Per*f*ume and *f*lowers *f*all in showers'. There is a discipline here, a discipline far more demanding, we might suppose, than that required for the writing of prose.

We have so far identified what Tennyson has written as poetry primarily by the form it has taken, without as yet needing to think about the subject matter. We have clear visual evidence of a rigorously ordered form of words, we have a verse structure of twelve lines, we have rhyme, and we have rhythm or metre. These are all attributes that will confirm us in our recognition of this as a poem. As yet, there has been no call on the reader necessarily to *understand* what has been written, and we might indeed go on to discuss the rhymes and metre used by Tennyson without touching upon any aspect of his meaning whatever. For example, there is an interesting variation of the rhyming pattern in the last four lines. The first eight lines form two groups of four:

```
. . . men                 . . . high
. . . sure                . . . steel
. . . ten                 . . . fly
. . . pure                . . . reel
```

At the end of the ninth line, however, the word 'lists' has no rhyming partner. The tenth and twelfth lines rhyme using 'stands' and 'hands', while the eleventh line, where we would have expected to find a mate for 'lists' has a rhyme within it:

They reel, they roll in clanging lists,
  And when the tide of combat <u>stands</u>,
Perfume and <u>flowers</u> fall in <u>showers</u>,
  That lightly rain from ladies' <u>hands</u>.

Such discoveries about a poem can never constitute an end in themselves, and how we might use this kind of information constructively will be illustrated in the chapters which follow. What we are discovering here is that our present way of defining poetry, of identifying 'poetic' qualities, may still leave us in total ignorance of the meaning; surely not a wholly satisfactory situation. Tennyson would certainly have been dissatisfied with praise based purely on his technical presentation, on his sensitive use of alliteration, for example, or his subtleties of rhyme. We must now therefore consider the subject and its meaning.

The meaning of most poetry is often thought to be, by definition, obscure or difficult, and certainly it is not clear at the outset of this verse that its specific subject is the prowess of Sir Galahad at tournaments. Obscurity, however, may be carefully contrived for a good reason, and is not necessarily a consequence of inadequate thought or knowledge on the part of the writer. Let us look closely at the way Tennyson fully reveals his whole subject by way of considering how poetry may operate fruitfully through an intended manipulation of obscurity.

The first line of the verse, 'My good blade carves the casques of men', indicates clearly that murderous sword-play is part of the subject. The second line, 'My tough lance thrusteth sure', implies medieval combat on horseback. To be sure of this we would of course need to know exactly what a lance was and how it was used. A degree of 'specialist' knowledge is therefore assumed. The testing of our vocabulary in this way is indicative of a literary quality more commonly associated with poetry than prose. Often we will find that certain information is left for the reader to supply; there will almost inevitably be certain things we have to work out for ourselves from clues, or hints, or types of words used. 'Casque' for helmet and 'lance' confirm the historical period of this poem. Scene setting of a detailed kind may legitimately be set to one side by the poet, who is more concerned to communicate immediate sense impressions. Tennyson is consciously making us work through our intellect and imagination to meet him on his way towards unfolding the meaning of his poem. We are actively involved in the composition.

It is as if we were invited not just to look at a painting of a tournament, but to step bodily into the real thing. While we might be happy to view the bloody combat from afar, actually becoming a part of it would be an intimidating option for most people; it would not just be the fact that it might be our midriff that gets a lance through it, we would be entering a period we were not at home in, one with a difficult vocabulary and strange manners, not to mention the mode of dress!

It is not until the use of the word 'lists' in the ninth line that we realize – if we know our tournament terminology – that the battles described are after all taking place in the context of a contrived sporting event, where ladies are watching from the safety of their ringside seats, throwing perfume and flowers to the victors.

On the first reading, therefore, the verse is bound in some respects to have an unfocused quality about it, but it is a lack of focus which enables the poet to create a very positive effect elsewhere. By refusing to give us date, time and place, and perhaps an historical gloss of Sir Galahad's place in Arthurian legends, Tennyson engages all the more directly his readers' basic emotions and feelings:

The shattering trumpet thrilleth high,
  The hard brands shiver on the steel,

Before we can set it in a safely distanced historical or mythical context, it is happening all around us, and we react directly to the sense of danger, excitement and furious activity, not realizing even that it is a kind of 'game'. But there is a price to pay for this vivid experience, and if we are at all of a practical disposition, and like to know exactly where we are and who is who before reading on, then it may seem a very high price to pay.

Our discussion of *Sir Galahad* has produced a reasonable amount of evidence that we might use to help us define poetry. The nature of the evidence is such that we may divide it into two categories. In the first place we were concerned with matters of formal presentation; clearly they were of some significance, but we saw also that there might be cause to question the extent to which they could really help us. Secondly the discussion moved on to consider how the subject of the verse was made apparent to the reader, and we then began to consider specifically poetic qualities of a very different order in Tennyson's work.

Now let us combine for a moment our study of specific issues of technique with the more general matter of Tennyson's carefully controlled presentation of his subject. If we look back from the effect achieved by the latter, it is certainly arguable that the poet's technique – his use of rhyme and rhythm, his very careful choice of words – positively assists him in achieving that effect, which is to intensify our immediate experience of his subject, rather than to establish a clear but distanced portrayal of a medieval scene.

Of one thing we may be sure. There are abundant reasons available to us for arguing that Tennyson is writing poetry when he writes *Sir Galahad*. I suspect that among the strongest of those will still be the fact that *Sir Galahad looks* like a poem, and whether we feel we understand it or not, its rhythms, its rhymes and its diction make it *sound* like a poem.

How do we respond, then, to the following extract from a poem by Adrian Mitchell (born 1932) called *Nostalgia – Now Threepence Off?*

Some failed. Desperate Dan and Meddlesome Matty and Strang
the Terrible and Korky the Cat killed themselves with free
gifts in a back room at the Peter Pan Club because they
were impotent, like us. Their audience, the senile Chums
of Red Circle School, still wearing for reasons of loyalty   5
the tatters of their uniforms, voted that exhibition a
super wheeze.
    Some succeeded. Tom Sawyer's heart has cooled, his
ingenuity flowers at Cape Canaveral.
    But they are all trodden on, the old familiar faces, so   10
at the rising of the sun and the going down of the ditto I
remember I remember the house where I was taught to play
up play up and play the game though nobody told me what
the game was, but we know now, don't we, we know what the
game is, but lives of great men all remind us we can make   15
our lives sublime and departing leave behind us arseprints
on the sands of time, but the tide's come up, the castles
are washed down, where are they now, where are they, where
the deep shelters? There are no deep shelters. Biggles may
drop it, Worrals of the Wraf may press the button. So,   20
Billy and Bessy Bunter, prepare for the last comic Yarooh
and throw away the Man-Tan. The sky will soon be full of
suns.
    (*BP*, pp. 303–5)

If we were left guessing in certain respects by Tennyson, the same must surely be true of Mitchell. The two extracts have this in common, the reader is expected to be drawn into making an effort to be clear about what is being said. Enough *is* understandable to hold our attention and make us want to know more.

The similarities between these two poems are in fact far greater than we might at first suppose. The verse from Tennyson's poem had references to things we should recognize: swords, lances and trumpets. It referred to things described in such a way as to set them in a specific period: 'casques' for example for helmets, and the 'lists' for a jousting field. Both indicate the medieval setting. Finally, of course, there is the reference to Sir Galahad himself, which might set in train a whole series of associations for the reader, or simply stir vague memories of Arthurian story-books long since abandoned.

The three paragraphs by Mitchell are full of references, all of them likely to require us to remember things from our past: Tom Sawyer, Billy Bunter, Biggles and Worrals of the Wraf. Recognizing some or all of these names as part of our own experiences during our formative years, we might be expected to want to know what they are doing there. Equally, if we recall Remembrance Day parades, we will be familiar with the phrase 'at the rising of the sun . . .'. We may also recall a poem with the words 'I remember, I remember/The house where I was born'.

Both poets, it seems, are using what they hope will be information or material familiar to us to manoeuvre us towards new experiences. Both extracts are a mixture of the strange and the familiar. Although Mitchell's poem is obviously set on dispelling the hallowed atmosphere created by 'poetic' words like 'thrilleth' and 'thrusteth' – he uses an ironically crude coinage like 'arse-prints' and talks of castles as being 'washed down' – his poem, like Tennyson's, will remain unfocused without our active participation to find its meaning.

The immediate appearance of the two poems is the first and most obvious difference between them. Tennyson is using verses, Mitchell writes in paragraphs and denies us a reassuring visual order underpinned by rhyme. As we found with *Sir Galahad*, even if the meaning was not clear, we could at least find something to say about structure. Mitchell has decided not to use any of the traditional poetic structures. His use of language, however, is clearly specialized; it is not the language of orthodox prose. His use of paragraphs has not meant the use of orthodox sentence structures; they run into each other so that the ideas and images seem to exist simultaneously rather than in an ordered sequence.

As with Tennyson's poem, we have investigated the claims of Mitchell's work to be poetry so far without beginning seriously to consider what it might actually mean. In doing so it has become apparent that *Nostalgia – Now Threepence Off* is asking for a special degree of commitment from the reader to discover its meaning. The consequence of that commitment will be that our experience of the piece will be intensified. We will have become far more involved in what is being said than we would have had we read a carefully explicit account of the lost innocence of childhood and the destructive evils of modern life: Tom Sawyer is now at Cape Canaveral, Biggles cannot wait to set the nuclear holocaust underway.

Part of our task as readers of poetry is to experience for ourselves the irony of 'I remember I remember the house where I was taught to play up play up and play the game though nobody told me what the game was . . .' (ll.11–14).

The first part of that passage is from a nostalgic nineteenth-century poem about childhood by Thomas Hood; a poem which at one time was certainly high on the list of poems to be learnt by heart and chanted together by classrooms of children. The quotation from this poem runs on into a cliché associated with the public school ethos. We are challenged to consider the two things as part of the same experience, even as they are here part of the same phrase. Beneath the reassuring sentimental image of the child at home, lurks the picture of children in serried ranks behind school desks (belonging no doubt to a school 'house' system) having opinions and prejudices rigidly drummed into them. For this to work, Mitchell has to assume that the sentiment of 'play up play up and play the game' will have long since lost credibility for his readers. He then hurries us on to his own final suggestive comment, that no one actually ever explained what the 'game' was, it was 'learnt' parrot-fashion like Hood's poem. He is evidently questioning established morality, and he wants us to participate in the discovery that it is to be questioned, not just to come away from his poem knowing what his view of the matter is.

It should be pointed out that Mitchell is doing no more than substituting one form of propaganda for another. Nor, for that matter, is *Sir Galahad* a disinterested piece of writing. Tennyson clearly wishes us to concur with his explicit approval of what Sir Galahad stands for: 'My strength is as the strength of ten / Because my heart is pure.' Galahad is of course playing his 'game' (a war-game no less) at the tournament.

We have now added considerably to our stock of possible evidence in our attempt to find what the ingredients of poetry might be. This has involved us in approaching our poems in terms of their formal presentation, and in terms of their subject and meaning. Concentrating on the issue of meaning, we should be aware that there is an important distinction to be made. There is the discussion of precise meaning in the case of individual poems, and it is in that direction we have tended when considering Mitchell's poem; and there is the more general discussion of how meaning – whatever that meaning may be – is intended to be communicated.

As soon as we get involved in questions of precise meaning, Tennyson and Mitchell seem light years apart. But different as the two extracts are, indeed antagonistic as they may seem (surely Galahad in the lists and Wellington on the playing fields of Eton are one and the same) we have somehow to agree that both are poetry. The common ground is evident if we concentrate on the question of how poetic communication works.

Using two very different poems has therefore had very important implications for our task of defining poetry. All the predictable hallmarks of poetry we found in *Sir Galahad* (verse structure, rhyme, regular line length and metre) are apparently no sure guide. And if the definition of poetry depends on other things, then presumably we might eventually be in a position to say that in certain cases, despite finding words arranged in orthodox rhyming verse form, we are not necessarily reading poetry.

What does at this stage appear to have been firmly established is that a poet will be using language in such a way as to bring the reader into a state of heightened awareness; he or she will be wanting to intensify the reader's sensitivity, almost to the point of making sense impressions and emotions seem actual. When thinking in these terms about poetry, it is almost inevitable that we should turn to John Keats for an example. These are the closing lines from his poem *Ode: To Autumn* (1819):

Then in a wailful choir the small gnats mourn
  Among the river sallows, borne aloft
    Or sinking as the light wind lives or dies;
And full-grown lambs loud bleat from hilly bourn;
  Hedge-crickets sing; and now with treble soft
  The red-breast whistles from a garden croft;
    And gathering swallows twitter in the skies.
  (*PBRV*, pp. 282–3)

Many readers have found, and indeed still find, that Keats is somehow giving them the experience of an Autumn evening in these lines; it goes beyond mere description. The success of the poetry rests ultimately not with Keats's mastery of technique, but with the effect achieved.

Poets in all periods have clearly felt that the use of specific disciplines in writing are an effective way of manipulating language to create a heightened intensity of meaning. It is not then so much a matter of dispensing with orthodox prose forms that 'makes' a poem, as seeking by whatever means to extend the possibilities of language. If poets decide to abandon clarity in certain things, it should be because there are other things that they wish to make not only clear, but vividly intense.

What we have also begun to appreciate is that the poet must require a very particular degree of collusion from the reader. In some way the reader must undertake to work *with* the poet on the poem, and it becomes a crucial part of the poet's task to find ways of binding the reader to the poem, of drawing the reader in. Thomas Hood, in the poem we have already briefly met, attempts to do just this in a time-honoured way, through the use of nostalgia:

I remember, I remember
The house where I was born,
The little window where the sun
Came creeping in at morn

We are likely to be drawn into Hood's poem not out of a fascination for the poet's birthplace, but because he will be inciting in us a wish to indulge in comforting memories of the supreme sanctuary of our own childhood. The very neatness and security of the verse endorses the invitation.

A poem, then, seeks to establish a special relationship between writer and reader; and what readers of poetry must be prepared for are the demands that will consequently be made on them. We may, of course, approach poetry by identifying and analysing its technical presentation; but as we have already seen, that need not tell us anything of the meaning, and in itself does not constitute the poem, just a chosen medium.

The poet's choice of form is always important, and recognizing what those forms are, and appreciating what kind of opportunities they create for the poet to establish that special relationship with the reader will be an important and helpful concern. But it is not in the end what makes it poetry.

Poetry – by our present definition – can exist within the context of virtually all literary forms. The following passage from Charles Dickens's novel, *Dombey and Son*, Chapter XX (1848), shows the author looking for an effect of heightened awareness and – in this instance through the introduction of rhythmical word patterns – dissolving the always fragile barrier between poetry and prose:

Away, with a shriek, and a roar, and a rattle, from the town, burrowing among the dwellings of men and making the streets hum, flashing out into the meadows for a moment, mining in through the damp earth, booming on in darkness and heavy air, bursting out again into the sunny day so bright and wide; away, with a shriek, and a roar, and a rattle, through the fields, through the woods, through the corn, through the hay, through the chalk, through the mould, through the clay, through the rock, among objects close at hand and almost in the grasp, ever flying from the traveller, and a deceitful distance ever moving slowly within him: like as in the track of the remorseless monster, Death!

The intensity of our experience, as we read of Mr Dombey's train journey, is achieved because Dickens incorporates poetry into his novel. There are a good many passages in Dickens's novels which may properly be defined as poetry rather than prose, and indeed, many novelists have incorporated the linguistic techniques of poetry into their work.

If we have learnt nothing else from this brief quest for definitions, it is that appearances can be deceptive, especially so if we place too much reliance on the physical appearance of words on the page to help us identify poetry. What we can be certain of is that a poem is a literary form where words will be used in ways that seek to enhance and extend the possibilities of the subject matter, establishing in the process a special relationship between writer and reader. It is not surprising to discover, therefore, that an abiding concern of poets has been to understand and, where necessary, redefine the nature of their relationship to the reader, their 'audience'. In the chapters which follow, this question of audience identity will be a recurring theme, helping us as we consider the problems of reading poetry written in so many different styles since the sixteenth century.

2

READING
SIXTEENTH-CENTURY
POETRY

The poet . . . cometh to you with words sent in delightful proportion, either accompanied with or prepared for the well enchanting skill of music; and with a tale forsooth he cometh unto you; with a tale which holdeth children from play, and old men from the chimney corner.

(Sir Philip Sidney, *Apologie for Poetry*, 1598)

Much of what we read is a matter of personal choice. In the literature produced for hobbies this is self evident, and we would be outraged if we found ourselves denied reading matter designed to feed our enthusiasms. In normal circumstances the same is equally true of 'literature'. If we develop a liking for novels or poetry, it will be because we have discovered among our reading certain novels or poems which have impressed us – for whatever reason – more than others; and although we may wish to continue experimenting with different writers, styles or categories, our natural inclination will be to seek out the writing which suits us best.

The specific problem facing many, possibly most, readers of this book is that the right of reading poetry according to preference has been arbitrarily overriden by an examination or course syllabus. We have been issued with a list of titles the reading of which by implication is going to be 'good for us'. Before long we may well discover that some of these 'set books' are not at all what we would have chosen for ourselves. Where the poetry is concerned, this may well mean every item, quite simply because the novel is now the dominant literary form, and comparatively few people read poetry by choice. I say comparatively, because far more people do in fact read and write poetry than we may suppose.

For the reluctant student of literature, there is little that can be done to alleviate the unpleasant task. For the committed student there is much to be said for approaching untrodden or at best dimly perceived ground initially through a consideration of the relationship between poets and readers in the period when the poetry was written, for this is something that has changed dramatically over the years. The fact that poetry may not be our first choice as readers need not stop us considering the identity and motivation of those for whom it has been, and is. Should we come up against a poem that seems particularly abstruse or difficult (whether written in the distant past or in our own time) we would do well to consider the nature of the audience the poet is seeking.

By the end of the eighteenth century, for example, it was very evident to poets that their art was no longer the dominant literary mode of expression. Most of the poets from this period familiar to us – Blake, Wordsworth, Coleridge, Shelley – were not the choice of large numbers of the reading public. Byron, of course, did have phenomenal success, while sentimental ballads and narrative poems were ever popular; but novels were the coming thing. Wordsworth for one complained bitterly of current trends in literary taste:

The invaluable works of our elder writers, I had almost said the works of Shakespear and Milton, are driven into neglect by frantic novels, sickly and stupid German Tragedies, and deluges of idle and extravagant stories in verse.
(Preface to *Lyrical Ballads*, 1800, *WPW*, p. 735)

Wordsworth could regretfully reflect on the great poets of the past – here as elsewhere he cites the poet he often consciously compared himself to, John Milton – and conjure up a time past when everyone who read with any seriousness read poetry. The 1800 preface to *Lyrical Ballads* (a joint venture with Coleridge) was in effect an extended essay on how to read poetry, and it was a matter of deep concern to him that such an essay had become necessary. In Milton's day the assumption was that no such instruction would have been needed.

The problem of many twentieth-century students feeling in need of specialized instruction when it comes to reading poetry has in fact been in the making for some two hundred years! It was signalled by poets of the late eighteenth century seeking to keep in touch with a public the size of which was rapidly growing, the composition of which was radically diversifying. Here is how Wordsworth described it in the same essay:

For a multitude of causes unknown to former times are now acting
with a combined force to blunt the discriminating powers of the mind,
and unfitting it for all voluntary exertion to reduce it to a state of
almost savage torpor. The most effective of these causes are the great
national events which are daily taking place, and the encreasing
accumulation of men in cities, where the uniformity of their
occupations produces a craving for extraordinary incident which the
rapid communication of intelligence hourly gratifies.
    (*WPW*, p. 735)

Since that time poets have responded in many ways to this
problem, not always, of course, defining it in precisely the same
terms as Wordsworth. In part at least the tremendous diversifica-
tion of styles we now have is a consequence of the loss of a stable
readership schooled in the set standards of various poetic forms.

If we make our way back in time through the centuries from the
period of Wordsworth's first publications in the 1790s, we witness
a shrinking of the potential audience for literature, who may
increasingly be assumed to have had a similar educational
grounding, at the heart of which lay the study of classical literature. In consequence many of the difficulties we may now
encounter when we read a sonnet written by a sixteenth-century
poet would simply not have struck its contemporary readers as
problematic at all. The best analogy I can offer is with soap-opera
on the television. To viewers of such series, the twists and turns of
the plot do not represent genuine moments of surprise, and they
recognize (and no doubt find reassuring) well loved set-pieces,
while at the same time appreciating the way in which they may be
presented in superficially original guises. The same applied to
readers of sonnets in Shakespeare's day.

The love poem, for example, had its expected formulae; the
loved one was more beautiful than anything achieved in nature:

Shall I compare thee to a summer's day?
Thou art more lovely and more temperate:
Rough winds do shake the darling buds of May,
And summer's lease hath all too short a date
    (*PBEV*, p. 231)

The words are familiar to many, and are the first four lines of
sonnet 18 by Shakespeare. Nature (the summer's day, the buds of
May) is beautiful. But nature's beauty is not perfect: summer can
be too hot and it doesn't last, the buds of May are often accompanied by rough weather. The poet's love surpasses this limited
loveliness. Imagine the pleasure, therefore, that a reader might

have when Shakespeare decided to turn this formula upside down, and say that in all honesty his love is *surpassed* by the beauty of nature, the beauty to be found in coral, snow, roses and music. In the same way today our sense of order might be challenged by a film that seems to threaten our received notion of what makes for security, the villains winning, the good suffering. Yet in the end, even if it is only at the last minute, the longed-for resolution is after all achieved; and so it is by Shakespeare in the final two lines of his sonnet:

Sections *Rhymes*

My mistress' eyes are nothing like the sun;
Coral is far more red than her lips' red;
If snow be white, why then her breasts are dun;
If hairs be wires, black wires grow in her head.
I have seen roses damask, red and white,
But no such roses see I in her cheeks;
And in some perfume is there more delight
Than in the breath that from my mistress reeks.
I love to hear her speak, yet well I know
That music hath a far more pleasing sound;
I grant I never saw a goddess go;
My mistress when she walks treads on the ground:
And yet by heaven I think my love as rare
As any she belied by false compare.
(Sonnet No. 130)

The poet's love is indeed perfect in his own eyes, nature is a 'false compare', or false comparison, as were the 'darling buds of May' which are shaken in the wind.

Notice how the poem's structure, one of several formal patterns established, and closely adhered to during this period for the sonnet form, helps him make his point. The length of line was fixed, as was its rhythm. It contained 10 syllables with the stress falling on every other syllable beginning with the second, an arrangement based on the natural speech rhythms of every-day usage. Marking the short syllables ˘, and the stressed syllables ´, it is easy to scan the first line, dividing it up into five units:

My mís.trĕss' eýes.arĕ nóth.ĭng líke.thĕ sún;

The unit is called an 'iamb', five of which are called an iambic pentameter.

The rhythm, as with speech, was necessarily variable to avoid too sing-song an effect. The natural stress of 'Coral' at the beginning of the second line is a case in point; but behind the evenly stressed syllables of that word runs our sense of a controlling rhythm that reasserts itself for the remainder of the line. Just as the word coral disturbs the rhythmic order of the line, so the sense of the line is a disturbance of what would be expected. Normally the poet would claim that his mistress's lips surpassed the red of coral.

Where rhyme was concerned, tolerance was the order of the day, a variety of rhyming schemes becoming popular. As long as the poet provided in some way a contrasting, argumentative representation of his subject, he was left free to experiment.

Shakespeare uses three four-line verses which together form a single twelve-line unit. This is followed by a 'couplet', two rhyming lines, making up the standard fourteen-line structure. Until the couplet, the rhymes have been on alternate lines (as marked); the final two lines are drawn together by rhyme giving the effect of a quickening of tempo. In the first part of the poem we have to wait three lines for any of the rhymes to be resolved ('sun' in line one has to wait for 'dun' (dark) in line three; 'red' has to wait for 'head' and so on). For a comparison we might think of a 'who-dunnit' where for the most part we deal with the protagonists separately, until the final scene when they are all brought together by the great detective who in a dramatic moment reveals the mystery (and our faulty powers of deduction).

Shakespeare's potential readership was limited compared with what it would be now. Much has been written of the lively oral traditions in Elizabethan England which fostered a broadly-based cultural life, and as a playwright Shakespeare would certainly have enjoyed a diverse audience through the medium of the London stage. As a poet, however, he would be read by only a small, homogeneous group within London society drawn primarily from those at Court, the universities and the Inns of Court. Though this was was a tiny minority of the estimated five million population of England, it was a minority with significant power and influence in the political as well as the cultural life of the country. Arguably his task as a poet was made easier by the fact that he could gauge the expectations of his audience with considerable precision; life was therefore made easier for his audience then than now. What were those expectations?

A twentieth-century poet, Edward Lucie-Smith, has made the point that Elizabethan readers were not overly concerned with the immediate, emotional appeal of a poem: 'Their reverence was given, not to the narrowly romantic idea of "being moved" by a poem, but to the riches of the English tongue, and to the innumerable beautiful and ingenious things which could be made by using it' (*PBEV*, p. 15). I have already suggested that to read poetry with any real degree of satisfaction, we need to join with the poet in the creative act. This necessary pact between writer and reader is what Wordsworth had in mind when he referred to the loss of a 'voluntary exertion' on the part of the reading public.

When confronted with Elizabethan poetry, therefore, it is of real assistance to know that much of the poet's creativity is likely to be taken up with offering his readership the intellectual pleasure of exploring language: the possibilities of imagery, the sound of words, the juxtaposition of ideas. Shakespeare and his contemporaries were by no means less human, passionate, or prone to fits of introversion than people are in our own time; but the relationship of imaginative composition to that aspect of human nature has undoubtedly changed. Once again, we can locate a significant period of change and experiment in that relationship with the latter decades of the eighteenth century. Robert Browning (1812–89), an avid student of the sixteenth century, wrote a poem in which he discusses the contrast between what was expected of poets then, and of himself writing in the nineteenth century.

The poem is a response to a comment on Shakespeare: 'With this same key [the sonnet form] Shakespeare unlocked his heart'. He begins by offering to use the sonnet himself to reveal his whole personality:

Shall I sonnet-sing you about myself?
  Do I live in a house you would like to see?
Is it scant of gear, has it store of pelf?
  'Unlock my heart with a sonnet-key?'

Invite the world, as my betters have done?
  'Take notice: this building remains on view,
Its suites of reception every one,
  Its private apartment and bedroom too . . .'

Browning himself is opposed to this contemporary idea of poetry. The poem should reveal as much of the poet as the poet chooses; the audience should take what is offered. It is the poem they should pry into, not seek to use it as simply a means to pry into his private life.

The poet may be thought of as a house; the public, his readers, have the right to view the outside only. Browning finishes with a rebuff to those who would suggest that all poets should reveal the inmost depths of their personalities through their work. Such is not the right relationship between poet and reader, even as it was not the relationship between Shakespeare and his readers:

'Hoity toity! A street to explore,
Your house the exception! *"With this same key*
Shakespeare unlocked his heart," once more!'
Did Shakespeare? If so, the less Shakespeare he!
   (Browning, *House*)

Living in the post-Romantic period, Elizabethan poetry may seem strangely impersonal to us, a quality we may or may not find attractive. As we read the love poetry of the period it will soon become apparent that actual passion for a real mistress was by no means a prerequisite for writing lavish praise of a loved one; we might as well demand that as require that no architect design a house unless he needs to live in it himself. If this impersonality (we may even consider it insincerity) is a stumbling block to our reading of Elizabethan poetry, it may well relate – as Browning had realized – to a more general problem of knowing how we as readers should relate to a poet's work. Analysing the sixteenth-century literary context can help us discuss that issue as much with regard to our response to later poetry as to that of the sixteenth century.

Renaissance literature in England constitutes a high point of cultural evolution that dated back to the 'Middle English' period which followed the Norman Conquest of 1066. If the late eighteenth and early nineteenth centuries constitute a watershed in English literary history with the growth of a larger, more diversified reading public, the establishment of a Norman king and court in the eleventh century heralded an even more fundamental process of cultural change. The rhythms of speech natural to the Germanic Anglo-Saxon tongue were overlaid by the iambic tendencies of French.

In Chapter 1 we established that a poet seeks to use language in the most effective way possible. His means of doing this will be governed by the nature of the language – the raw material – available to him. Subtleties of meaning associated with individual words, grammatical constructions and speech rhythms created by the language will all act as controls.

With the influx of Norman–French influences on language and culture, there began a profound linguistic and cultural revolution, not least because language was becoming a written medium, whereas before it had been primarily oral. The goals of earlier poets as they strove to perfect expression no longer applied to poets who were handling the new medium. Natural speech rhythms were altering, the nature of words changed, and as fashions of dress also changed, so at a deeper level were notions of excellence and perfection changing with the introduction of feudalism. This was a process that took place over a long period of time, of course; there was no single moment of dramatic change, and indeed it is still possible to trace native, Anglo-Saxon influences in much sixteenth-century English poetry. The contrast, however, between 'Old English' pre-conquest poetry and, for example, the Shakespeare already quoted, is very clear. For one thing, where rhyme is clearly central to the order and control evident in a Shakespeare sonnet, earlier poets sought the same effect through alliteration. Their native tongue was manifestly well suited to the task:

   Now come thoughts
Knocking my heart, of the high waves,
clashing salt-crests, I am to cross again.
Mind-lust maddens, moves as I breathe
soul to set out, seek out the way
to a far folk-land flood-beyond.
   (*The Seafarer, EEP*, p. 75)

The 'modern' English poet of the sixteenth century, for whom pre-Norman Old English would have seemed almost as archaically strange a language as it does to us, had Italian, French, Latin and Spanish models of poetry – language in its most refined and civilized contemporary form – to respond to. Alliteration was far from being banished completely, and in the poetry of Edmund Spenser (1552–99), we may see ample evidence of his mastery of the sonnet form, an Italian import, while at the same time in his major work, a long poem called *The Faerie Queene*, he devised his own stanza form, every bit as demanding as the sonnet from the point of view of rhyme, yet equally sustained by what for him was a contrived recreation of the language and alliteration of earlier times. Here is Spenser with a sophisticated sonnet that rehearses in the appropriate manner the theme of mortal transience and the eternal nature of love and art:

One day I wrote her name upon the strand,
But came the waves and washèd it away:

Again I wrote it with a second hand,
But came the tide and made my pains his prey.
Vain man, said she, that dost in vain assay,
A mortal thing so to immortalise,
But I myself shall like to this decay,
And eke my name be wipèd out likewise.
Not so (quod I), let baser things devise
To die in dust, but you shall live by fame:
My verse your virtues rare shall enternise,
And in the heavens write your glorious name.
   Where whenas death shall all the world subdue,
   Our love shall live, and later life renew.
     (*PBEV*, p. 250)

In *The Faerie Queene* Spenser sought to captivate his audience by an extended tribute to the glories of England under Queen Elizabeth, using as his setting the mythical times of King Arthur. Here the Red Crosse Knight has severly wounded his foe, a terrifying dragon. The alliteration has been indicated as well as the demanding rhyme scheme:

He cryde, as *r*aging seas are wont to *r*ore,
  *W*hen *w*intry storme his *w*rathfull *w*reck does threat,
  The *r*olling *b*illowes *b*eat the *r*agged shore,
  As they the earth would shoulder from her seat,
  And *g*reedie *g*ulfe does *g*ape, as he would eat
  His neighbour element in his revenge:
  Then gin the *b*lustring *b*rethren *b*oldly threat,
  To move the world from off his steadfast henge,
And *b*oystrous *b*attell make, each other to avenge.
    (*The Faerie Queene*, Book I, stanza xxi)

Spenser had provided originality through the concoction of a stanza form that was subsequently to be named after him. Yet he also fascinated his readers with his mock-medieval language and word order. He looked back not so much to the period of *The Seafarer* as to the Middle English poetry of Langland (1330–1400?) and Chaucer (1345–1400) which retained close links with the earlier Anglo-Saxon roots of language. The expertise of a contemporary poet is clearly apparent elsewhere in *The Faerie Queene* through constant references to classical images culled from poets revered at the time; but the use of much older idioms and words provided the patriotic ring that Spenser – ever hopeful of political preferment – sought from his Queen.

In all this we may begin to appreciate more about the sixteenth-century poet and his audience. One generally accepted view of the

Elizabethans is their sense of themselves as living in a 'golden age'; it was a time of intense national pride, symbolized polit- ically and economically by the defeat of the Spanish Armada in 1588. What their literature celebrated was an ideal of social perfection, and a new English language was only then emerging as the medium fit to give expression to this ideal. Where previously Latin had been the common language of all educated Europeans, now English began to challenge that dominance. English writers, convinced of their country's superiority in everything else, forged new words, adapted and enlarged old ones, and generally encour- aged a heady enthusiasm for a new, burgeoning language fit for all purposes and second to none.

In 1598 George Chapman, for example, defended his English translation of Homer's *Iliad* at length, claiming boldly that his native tongue was far superior to French or Italian for writing poetry:

> . . . I can prove it clear
> That no tongue hath the Muses' utterance heired
>   For verse and that sweet music for the ear
> Struck out of rhyme, so naturally as this;
>   Our monosyllables so kindly fall
> And meet, opposed in rhyme, as they did kiss;
>   French and Italian, most immetrical;
> Their many syllables, in harsh collision,
>   Fall as they brake their necks; their bastard rhymes
> Saluting as they justled in transition,
>   And set our teeth on edge; nor tunes, nor times
> Kept in their falls. And methinks, their long words
>   Show in short verse, as in a narrow space
> Two opposites should meet, with two-hand swords
>   Unwieldly, without or use or grace.
>   (*PBEV*, p. 67)

For Chapman the wheel has come full circle. Italian and French, the linguistic begetters of the renaissance in English Literature, are now become a hindrance. He was writing, we should always remember, in the certain knowledge that his audience would be familiar with his subject, the merits of language itself. They would be eager to participate in his poem as readers in a way we could not pretend to simulate. This one example is indicative of the way in which a sixteenth-century poet could be confident of his role in relation to his public to a degree which is impossible for a contemporary poet.

The realization of the individual Elizabethan's personality was
not expressed in individual, introverted terms, but projected onto
the broader canvas of the perfection of the state, or commonwealth. The highest, most civilized form that art could take was
therefore one that expressed this general view. Personal love and
affection, while it obviously existed, was not the stuff of art. The
love of individuals for each other passes away, love as a general
principle does not. Time and again, sixteenth-century poets
expressed variations on this theme:

How many paltry, foolish, painted things,
That now in coaches trouble every street,
Shall be forgotten, whom no poet sings,
Ere they be well-wrapped in their winding sheet?
(Michael Drayton 1563–1631, *PBEV*, p. 105)

The sonnet was of course not the only verse form that came to be
associated with this notion of art at its most civilized, but in many
ways it serves as an excellent indication of prevailing cultural
expectations. Poets could use it in the confidence that their
limited audience (most of whom would be writing sonnets also)
would be familiar with its demands. Its brevity demanded technical skill and precision of expression, and it allied writers, and by
implication the society that had produced them, to literary figures
who had come to be revered and associated with politically mature
civilizations. At the same time it distanced the art of an earlier
barbaric and supposedly scarcely civilized era before the Norman
Conquest. With the intimate atmosphere that the limited
audience of this period produced, highly specialized art forms
could flourish. There need be no anxiety about not being understood by large sections of the reading public.

Sonnets are still written; the particular discipline of the
fourteen-line poem can still appeal to poets, depending upon
what they have it in mind to say. One such twentieth-century poet
was W.H. Auden:

*Embassy**

As evening fell the day's oppression lifted;
Far peaks came into focus; it had rained:
Across wide lawns and cultured flowers drifted
The conversation of the highly trained.

* Auden continually revised and reworked his poetry. The text used here comes
from an edition of his poems he edited for *Penguin Poets* (London, Penguin,
1958), p. 57.

Two gardeners watched them pass and priced their shoes:
A chauffeur waited, reading in the drive,
For them to finish their exchange of views;
It seemed a picture of the private life.

Far off, no matter what good they intended,
The armies waited for a verbal error
With all the instruments for causing pain:

An on the issue of their charm depended
A land laid waste, with all its young men slain,
Its women weeping, and its towns in terror.

Auden here follows closely – though not precisely – the rhyming scheme of the Latin poet Petrarch (1304–74), whose sonnets formed the original model for sixteenth-century poets. He augments orthodox iambic scansion with the two-syllable rhyming words at the end of the first and third, ninth and twelfth, tenth and fourteenth lines; the effect is to tighten the sense of overall order throughout the poem. The lines are welded more firmly together by 'lifted' / 'drifted', than by 'rained' / 'trained'.

Embassy is a brief, trenchant comment on the contrast between the unreal world of diplomacy, a world of contrived, expensive beauty symbolized by the carefully maintained house and garden; and the harsh, real world which must suffer the consequences of wrong or imperfect decisions taken, or indeed decisions imprecisely expressed. Between the two worlds is a gulf of incomprehension. The scene at the Embassy seems 'a picture of the private life'; something, in other words, which keeps itself to itself, having no direct contact with or proper knowledge of matters in the outside world. The final three lines expose the bitter consequences of this dangerous ignorance. It is not intended as a poem which suggests a solution, it simply seeks to expose as starkly as possible the state of affairs.

The sonnet form is ideally suited to Auden's purpose. The Petrarchan model divides its two potentially contrasting sections between the first eight and the last six lines ('octet' and 'sestet'). The issue must be stated briefly, and brevity along with the precision of the rhyming scheme and scansion is central to the poem's effect. The mannered nature of sonnet writing, a self-consciously 'artistic' exercise, is particularly relevant to the impression Auden is striving for in the first section of the poem: an artificial, mannered world. Equally important, and part of the tradition of sonnet writing as we have seen, is the impersonality of the sonnet writer. The sonnet helps Auden here give an apparently clinical, objective account of the subject. This is maintained throughout the poem, where the restraint evident in Auden's method of description is particularly effective in the second section. Here we find him using diplomatic language to describe things too uncomfortable to be spoken of frankly within the Embassy world of 'wide lawns and cultured flowers'. Guns, tanks and bombs become 'instruments for causing pain'. The irony is sharp indeed.

What we are now aware of is that a twentieth-century poet has found the most suitable style for his poem in a poetic form established in the sixteenth century, albeit his sonnet is in many ways a very different poem from that which an Elizabethan would have set out to write. Where Auden is obviously in a very different position from his sixteenth-century forbears is in his relationship to his audience. We have been able to appreciate something of the nature of a sixteenth-century reader's position in relation to English poetry. He belonged to a literate minority who were thoroughly familiar with the medium of poetry, and would certainly have had no need to discuss technical details in the way we so often do. To such a reader, sonnet form would have been second nature. My brief reading of *Embassy* has been sustained by academic points of reference stemming from our comparative unfamiliarity with the form; I have had of necessity to refer back to the rules of a game which flourished when poetry and its readership enjoyed a very different relationship. This specialized knowledge was not crucial to my being able to get at the poem's meaning, but it did enable me to appreciate that meaning to the full. My ability to recognize the implications of Auden's deliberate choice of sonnet form created that all-important partnership between myself as reader, and Auden as poet. Just as that choice, with its now academic as well as artistic significances, was part of the poet's creative act of composition, so my ability to recognize it enriched my appreciation of the poem.

Discussing a twentieth-century poem like *Embassy* serves to highlight a problem for modern poets and readers virtually non-existent in the sixteenth century. A twentieth-century readership is not prepared, quite literally not educated, for its poetry in the way an Elizabethan readership was. In the case both of form and subject matter this should have become clear, helping us at least to understand why reading early poetry may present the difficulties it does, even if it does not always begin to solve them.

One further obstacle may now be considered. The enthusiasm of the Elizabethans for the evolving riches of their own native language, meant that the literate were acutely aware of its sounds and rhythms. Poets could therefore use this awareness to help them

create the effects they sought. The modern reader can hardly fail
to notice the presence of alliteration in Spencer, although the full
effect of that alliteration may have to be more carefully pointed
out; but without an informed effort we may very easily miss other
more subtly deployed rhythms and sounds that delighted the ear
of an earlier readership. To illustrate this I shall take two stanzas
from a poem praising Sir Thomas Wyatt (1503–42) by Henry
Howard, Earl of Surrey (1517–47). Both men were instrumental
in shaping sixteenth-century taste in poetry, and were largely
responsible for convincing their readership of the virtues of sonnet
form as a vehicle for English poetry. Surrey describes Wyatt thus:

A visage stern and mild, where both did grow,
Vice to contemn, in virtue to rejoice;
Amid great storms, whom grace assured so,
To live upright, and smile at fortune's choice.
    (*SP*, p. 141)

Surrey uses the ten syllable, iambic metre we have already met.
This gives him his basic framework. The phrasing, marked out by
the punctuation, is complemented by the overall control of his
line structure. In consequence we should be conscious of a pause
all the more acutely if it comes before the end of a line. Here each
line has a pause approximately mid-way through it. In the second
line it serves to emphasize the juxtaposition of vice and virtue,
reflecting the two sides of his character described in line one
within one phrase, 'stern and mild'. A reader hearing the sounds
of the words while reading would equally be conscious of the
explosive quality of '*st*ern' compared with the gentleness of
'*m*ild'. Similarly, in the third line we have the existence side by
side of '*st*orms', separated by a comma from the smooth sounds
accompanying 'grace', the soothing effect of '*grace assurèd so*'. It
is a verse of opposites reconciled within the one personality. The
division of each line into two, not allowing the natural unit of any
line to complete its iambic pentameter flow unchecked, creates a
tension in itself descriptive of Wyatt's complex personality.

The other verse deals not in contraries, rather it tells of the
power of Wyatt's rhetoric. Note how the punctuation indicates a
quite different effect:

A tongue that served in foreign realms his king;
Whose courteous talk to virtue did inflame
Each noble heart; a worthy guide to bring
Our English youth by travail unto fame.

The gift of 'courteous talk' lies not in abruptness, it flows; and the second line flows on into the third, when we are allowed to pause before being 'guided' through into the final line. The poetic rhythm of three lines is broadened out by Surrey's subdivision of them into two grammatical phrases. The general impression of the word sounds are smooth and beguiling. No consonants interrupt the break from line two to three, rather we have open vowel sounds: 'did inflame / Each noble heart'.

Surrey disturbs the iambic rhythm at two points. In the first verse quoted, the beginning of the second line would more naturally scan, 'Více tŏ.cŏntémn' (the first foot becoming a 'trochee', though the two feet work better when treated as a single unit of rhythm). The consequent awkwardness has its part to play in a complete reading of the poem in that the act described is of a disturbing nature. In the final line of the second verse quoted the stresses on the two syllables of 'travail' are more naturally even than long and short. Travail here means hard work or effort, and an effort is indeed required of the reader who must reconcile this word to the overall metrical structure of the poem.

'Reading' a poem in this way may seem a highly self-conscious exercise in technique, confirming our suspicion that poetry is indeed a highly specialized art form far removed from our normal habit of reading. What we must appreciate, however, is that the linguistic qualities we see Surrey here exploiting are not being newly created by 'poetry', rather they are inherent in language itself. The historic role of poetry has been the perfection of expression; poems from any period may deal in trivia, there has always been room for 'light verse', but at the other end of the scale the most *complete* expression of truth requires the medium of poetry precisely because it synthesizes every existing facet of linguistic expression.

The situation we are faced with in our own century is one where the fundamental definition of poetry has not changed, but the circumstances in which poets function most certainly has, virtually beyond recognition. Poets continue to write with a heightened sensitivity towards language, but that sensitivity is no longer equally in the possession of the poet's audience. The complicity between writer and reader so important to the poet cannot be guaranteed.

Perhaps the most damaging consequence of the resulting uncertainty for the poet in this situation, is the temptation to meet a sense of impending isolation with a positive act of self-isolation; of deliberate obscurity and obfuscation.

T.S. Eliot's *The Waste Land* (1922) is probably the poem most

frequently singled out as an example of the poet actually seeking
to ward off a wide readership, inviting instead a few scholarly
minds to decipher the product of a cultured, erudite mind. Eliot's
theme is the breakdown of cultural values and standards in the
modern world, and what he seems to be saying to most readers is
that they are ignorant, too ignorant even to be helped by his footnotes. Where footnotes normally give us a helping hand with
obscurity, Eliot's seem designed to deliver the final blow to what
self confidence we may have had. His notes on Section I of the
poem ('The Burial of the Dead'), for example, include a reference
to *'Tristan und Isolde'* (pay careful attention to the 'und',
presumably translations are not permitted). We could of course
seek it out, but to be referred to that poem, and subsequently to
Dante, Virgil, Duessen's *Sechzig Upanishads des Veda*, and to
have nineteen untranslated lines of Ovid quoted at us, may seem
a strategy designed as much to bring us to our knees in despair as
to enlighten us. (See *The Waste Land,* p. 64 ll.31–42 and
pp. 80–6.*)

The fact remains, of course, that *The Waste Land* is a poem
which continues to draw readers to it; partly, no doubt, because it
was officially identified as 'important' by the literary establishment of the time, but equally because it does undeniably possess a
quality that intrigues and fascinates even as it seems to repel our
attempts to understand it fully.

Extreme case it may be, *The Waste Land* is nevertheless indicative of how poets writing in our own time of mass literacy, and in
the midst of a bewilderingly fragmented set of cultural expectations, have found themselves forced to address limited audiences
of their own choice. The literate populace simply do not have the
aims, enthusiasms and educational background in common that
existed in the sixteenth century. An Elizabethan poet, for
example, might write enthusiastically on a patriotic theme, as
Spenser did at great length in *The Faerie Queene*, assuming the
general approval of his audience in a way that poets – even by
the end of the seventeenth century – certainly could not. An
important ingredient of Adrian Mitchell's poem, *Nostalgia –
Now Threepence Off*, is, as we have seen, its attack on the
patriotic jingoism inculcated into children through school, and
through fiction like W.E. Johns's *Biggles* stories. Yet there is a

---

* Eliot's poetic form for *The Waste Land* is 'free verse'. This is discussed in
Chapter 4. A helpful account of the immediate context of *The Waste Land* and the
reasons for its impact on British poetry will be found in James Reeve's introduction
to *Georgian Poetry* (London, Penguin, 1981), pp. xi–xxiii.

sense in which Mitchell's satire can only work properly for that section of society who know about – or even went to – the appropriate type of school, and who were captivated by the exploits of
Biggles in their youth. In this respect, Mitchell – like Auden
with his sonnet – is to some extent selecting his audience.

One consequence for the poet of this breakdown of homo-
geneity in society has been the tendency for a greater degree of
introversion. In the absence of a coherent 'social' subject, the poet
himself becomes of necessity increasingly his own subject whose
function – notably in the late eighteenth century – was to
offer a unifying vision of a divided world.

More often than not an Elizabethan poet would bring a unified
social ideal to bear on his own, divided, consciousness. In love
poetry, for example, there were well-established social conventions; where they failed to conform with personal experience,
these conventions could then be used to stabilize the individual's
confusion. The modern love poem will often contrast with
sixteenth-century poems of this genre by being unashamedly intimate. The resolution of a Shakespeare love poem is simply impossible for the modern poet. It is not so much a matter of those
conventions being at one time a true reflection of the way things
were in reality, simply that then they were widely acceptable as an
ideal, whereas now they are not. By way of an example, we may
consider *The Bruise*, by Edward Lucie-Smith (born 1933):

The ghost of your body
Clings implacably to
Mine. When you are absent
The air tastes of you, and
Last night the sheets had your
Texture. Then, when I looked
In this morning's mirror,
I found a bruise which had
Suddenly risen through
The milky flesh, a black
Star on the breast, surely
Not pinned there before (I
Count my wounds, and record
The number). How did it
Arrive? The ghost made it.
I turn, hearing you laugh.
    (*British Poetry*, p. 209)

The individual's circumstances are only too clear. The lover is
gone, the relationship terminated. Yet the pain of love remains,

no less real for its disembodied 'ghostly' form. In place of the generalized resolution we might expect from an Elizabethan poem, however, we are left with a taunting, unresolved, ghostly laugh. It is for each individual reading this poem to understand it according to their personal experience of intimate relationships. There is no appeal to any generalized convention of how the situation may be interpreted and thus dealt with. We have only the integrity of the poet's own experience to go by. If we doubt the truth of his narration, the poem loses credibility. The Elizabethan poet we know felt no such constraints to abide by that kind of honesty.

The stand-point of the poet in relationship to his readership has indeed changed, and the result is a very different kind of poem from that previously possible. *The Bruise* is, nevertheless, a poem. It is an exploration through language in search of the most effective means of expressing its subject, and the fact that it appears in a form far less predictable than the poetry of Surrey, Spenser or Shakespeare need not intimidate us if we wish (or should be required) to read it with a view to close analysis.

Lucie-Smith has evidently rejected rhyme as a technique that will suit his purpose, but the poem is carefully structured despite that. A careful reading – preferably aloud – should confirm the visual impression that line length is constant. We can check this simply enough by counting syllables; there are six to each line. Here then is an important element of the poem's structure. What we now have to do is look at how the poet is using his regular line length. Surrey's lines fell naturally into iambic feet, the first line of the poem's second verse will illustrate this:

Ă héad.whĕre wís.dŏm mýs.tĕriés.dĭd fráme;

We would not necessarily wish to emphasize the beat, but if we listen to where we are naturally inclined to place emphasis, we may appreciate that Surrey's composition has been informed by a desire to establish an iambic pattern within his ten syllable line.

Lucie-Smith's lines have no such tendency, and to impose iambic rhythm upon them would render them nonsensical. Using the standard symbols, a natural reading of the first sentence of *The Bruise* would approximate to:

Thĕ ghóst ŏf yoŭr bódў
Clíngs ĭmplácabłў tŏ
Míne.

There is no regularity in the spacing of short and long stresses, but
if we continue as above, we would find that a regular pattern of
two long stresses in each line emerges. This loose but definite
form of rhythmical structure brings the line much closer to the
vagaries of stress in normal speech. The technical name for it is
'sprung rhythm', where we have a rhythmic unit (or foot) of not
more than four syllables, one of which is stressed. Probably the
best known exponent of sprung rhythm was Gerard Manley
Hopkins (1844–89).

Choosing words for each line to maintain this structure helps
Lucie-Smith give his reader (a reader as always who is fully
prepared to take an active part in his poem) the clearest sense
possible of the experience he wishes to communicate. The stress
on the one word 'Clings', for example, with the second stress in
the line diminished by being embedded in the four syllables of
'implacably', has the effect of dramatically enacting the
meaning.

Given the regular line length, the poet is in a position to do the
same as Surrey, to use that underlying regularity to manipulate
where emphases come. The run-on from line one to line two helps
emphasize the stress on 'Clings', and the run-on from line two to
line three builds to an even more dramatic climax on 'Mine'. The
natural place to end a sentence is at the end of the line; to do so at
the beginning of a line has an effect analogous to a discord in
music where concordance is the established mode. Once we are
aware of this, we can see him operating this technique repeatedly:

I foúnd a brúise which had
Súddenly . . .
       . . . a bláck
Stár on the bréast . . .
       . . . Hów did it
Arrive?

Worth commenting on in this respect is the fact that the first and
last lines are virtually self-sustaining. The poem therefore begins
and ends with a clear indication of its underlying, controlling line
length.

Being able to use the relevant technical terminology has clearly
helped us in this discussion; but knowledge of that terminology in
recent times has lapsed, and this is one mark of the difference
between our own society and that of a sixteenth-century reader of
poetry. The latter was part of a sufficiently homogeneous cultural
world to know at once the formal name tags and what they meant.

Far more important, however, has been the way we have been able (through the medium of such terminology) to discuss sixteenth-century poetry alongside modern poetry. Though the poems of the different periods have proved very unlike, it should be clear that the fundamental skills required to develop an analysis are the same.

The real problem we face in reading *The Bruise*, stems from the fact that while the basic relationship of poetry to language and meaning has remained the same, its interrelationship with its readership has shifted to such an extent that the challenge of writing and reading poetry *is* significantly altered. The poet confronts an audience which has a wide variety of options, and, as we saw at the beginning of the chapter, every opportunity and right to exercise a choice. The reader of poetry is faced with a remarkably varied range of poetic composition which exists in a literary climate where poetry has long since ceased to hold its place as the primary literary form, and where awareness and sensitivity to language is experienced in ways which no longer guarantee a confident response to the art.

Such a situation, as we have seen, was already clearly recognizable in Wordsworth's time, and we must now consider in more detail the way poetry evolved from the early seventeenth century. In the process, I hope to show how poems from those various periods may be read and discussed.

3
POETRY IN A CHANGING WORLD

> In our halls is hung
> Armoury of the invincible Knights of old:
> We must be free or die, who speak the tongue
> That Shakespeare spake; the faith and morals hold
> Which Milton held.
>
> (Wordsworth, *Poems Dedicated to Natural Independence and Liberty*, Sonnet xvi)

In one of his poems, Thom Gunn (born 1929) describes an Elizabethan England rather different from the one my brief comments in Chapter 1 may have suggested. Here are the first three verses of *A Mirror for Poets*:

It was a violent time. Wheels, racks and fires
In every writer's mouth, and not mere rant.
Certain shrewd herdsmen, between twisted wires
Of penalty folding the realm, were thanked
For organising spies and secret police
By richness in the flock, which they could fleece.

Hacks in the Fleet and nobles in the Tower
Shakespeare must keep the peace, and Jonson's thumb
Be branded (for manslaughter), in the power
Of irons lay the admired Southampton.
Above all swayed the diseased and doubtful queen:
Her state canopied by the glamour of pain.

In this society the boundaries met
Of living, danger, death, leaving no space
Between, except where might be set
That mathematical point whose time and place
Could not exist. Yet at this point they found
Arcadia, a fruitful permanent land.
    (*TNP*, pp. 154–5)

It is not my intention to analyse in any detail Gunn's technique, what concerns us here is the point he is making. In the first instance, should any of his readers believe that life in the Elizabethan world was a matter of civilized pageantry at court, and dream-like pastoral happiness in the sunny countryside of that mythical land, Arcadia, then he wishes to disabuse them.

It was an insecure time when spies, informers and a secret police were kept very busy. Secondly, and most significantly, it was a time when poets and their poetry were an integral part of all that went on; a mistake could cost them dear: 'Wheels, racks and fires/In every writer's mouth'. The Arcadia of which they wrote was no more than a dream-world where they could imagine themselves safe from the caprices of a society ruled over by 'the diseased and doubtful queen'. Arcadia must exist if only because the everyday world was so inhospitable, but its existence might only ever be proved in theoretical terms, 'That mathematical point whose time and place/Could not exist'.

Having held up a mirror to the Elizabethan world, and found the poet to be in the centre of the reflection, Gunn then holds up a mirror to the society in which his own contemporaries are writing, and asks them if they stand where their predecessors stood. In the last verse of the poem he writes, 'I am myself, but part of something greater,/Find poets what that is . . .'. The poet, he says, should be 'a cruelly insistant friend/You cannot smile at me and make an end'.

For Shakespeare and his contemporaries to find themselves at odds with the authorities was commonplace. Their misdemeanours could range from a violent approach to settling personal vendettas (as with Ben Jonson), to the alleged political crimes of the Earl of Southampton. While nobles who dealt in politics and literature ended up in the Tower, 'hack' writers who readily did the same were dispatched to the Fleet prison. For Gunn this all points to a literature which lay far more at the centre of everyday life and society than is the case in his own time. Few would suggest that contemporary British poets, no matter how politically committed they might be, have to glance fearfully over their shoulders in quite the way Gunn suggests they did in the Elizabethan period.

In this respect poets might be thought to have suffered a considerable loss of authority. The change in the relationship between poet and reader which has accompanied this loss has inevitably affected the way we read poetry written in earlier times. There is now a tendency in criticism to rediscover the social and political cutting edge of poets who have otherwise been considered as individuals standing in some way independently from the major political issues of their day. But such an exercise remains to a significant degree academic. In the end we are bound to admit that the poet who attempts to become a real force in the shaping of public opinion will, as Gunn suggests, be considered a producer of 'mere rant'.

It would be wrong, of course, to suggest that it is entirely the poet's fault that this situation has come about. The changes in society, above all the fundamental changes that have occurred in the constitution of the reading public since the time Gunn is writing about, are forces beyond, it would seem, anyone's control. It might also be argued that poets have always been primarily concerned with human nature rather than overtly political matters, a concern which has led them to reflect deeply on the workings of their own minds rather than the desirability of a particular political policy. But I have already suggested that notions of the experience of individuals and the collective experience of society as a whole were viewed in a far more unified, organic light then than now. Poets of the sixteenth century who wrote as 'individuals' were not necessarily absenting themselves from society, rather they would be writing for a society which listened, understood, and might be expected to respond in collective terms. This is the difference, if you like, between a twentieth-century poet being attacked for his work by a reviewer in *The Times Literary Supplement,* and a sixteenth-century poet being sent to the Fleet!

It is very often language, unfamiliar syntax, obscurity of references, or unfamiliar images which are cited as the main reasons why the poetry of the past is difficult for the modern reader. There is no doubt that such things can prove awkward. But what we so often lack at the outset, and so desperately need if we are to grasp the poet's overall meaning, is the ability to place ourselves in something approximating to the position of the audience for whom the poem was meant. The general impression – and it may be no more than that – of what the poet wants to say, is our best aid to clarifying obscurity of expression caused by the period of the poem. This conviction is not infrequently rejected by the accomplished reader of poetry who would argue for the eternal relevance of great art. The fact is that such purists will be found to have the necessary scholarship to make the transition from sixteenth- to eighteenth- to twentieth-century audience awareness without any real conscious effort.

Sixteenth-century poetry was, as we have seen, profoundly influenced by classical culture. The belief that one should look to Italy for guidance in form and content continued on through the seventeenth century and into the eighteenth century. Indeed, such was the commitment of artists and their public to Italy as the fountain-head of civilization, that the period prior to the emergence of the 'Romantic Movement' has become known as 'Augustan', setting up the period of the Emperor Augustus (27BC–AD14) as its specific model.* Readers of the seventeenth century were not, however, content just to inherit a prepacked model of classical literature from their predecessors. New forms, along with experimentation with established ones, were emerging, partly because of a concern of a number of poets – despite a continued appreciation of translations – that English literature should develop a distinctive voice.

Poets of the first half of the seventeenth century were collectively referred to by the poet John Dryden (1631–1700) as 'Metaphysical', a term taken up with approval by Dr Johnson in the eighteenth century, and one which has since stuck. It signifies something of the changes that were taking place, drawing attention to the way poets searched for startling effects through unexpected though ultimately appropriate imagery, and the way they displayed their agility of intellect.

In one respect, however, there was little change from the previous century in that the poet's audience remained limited to the more privileged classes of society. The basic forms which poetry could take also remained more or less constant. The sonnet persisted, though somewhat less in fashion than previously; the epic, an extended narrative telling of the heroic exploits of its central character or characters was considered the highest form of poetic achievement; satire, in which the follies of the age were revealed and ridiculed, was becoming more popular; the extended philosophical meditation, usually described as an elegy (though it did not always lament a death) was considered a suitable vehicle for serious poetic expression; and of course there were 'songs', which were becoming in some cases increasingly complex in meaning and stylistically ornate, for the most part love poems written to be read or recited rather than sung.

Thomas Carew's elegy on the death in 1631 of one of the best known Metaphysical poets, John Donne, is a helpful indicator of the direction poetry was taking at this time. Carew lived from 1594/5 to 1640; this passage appears early in the poem.

* See Donald Davie's introduction to *TLA*, pp. vii–xxxiii

The Muses garden with Pedantique weedes
O'rspred, was purg'd by thee; The lazie seeds
Of servile imitation throwne away;
And fresh invention planted, Thou didst pay
The debts of our penurious bankrupt age;
Licentious thefts, that make poetique rage
A Mimique fury, when our soules must bee
Possesst, or with Anacreons Extasie,
Or Pindars, not their owne; The subtle cheat
Of slie Exchanges, and the jugling feat
Of two-edg'd words, or whatsoever wrong
By ours was done the Greeke, or Latine tongue,
Thou hast redeem'd, and open'd Us a Mine
Of rich and pregnant phansie, drawne a line
Of masculine expression, which had good
Old Orpheus seene, Or all the ancient Brood
Our superstitious fooles admire, and hold
Their lead more precious, than thy burnish't Gold,
Thou hadst been their Exchequer, and no more
They in each others dust, had rak'd for Ore.
(*TMP*, pp. 143–4)

Carew writes in couplets, that is to say, pairs of rhyming lines. This suggests a unit of expression, even as the line itself is a natural unit of expression. We have already seen the couplet used to good effect at the end of the Shakespearian sonnet. Through constant use of 'enjambment' (the carrying over of one line into the next), Carew challenges the authority of the technical structure of the poem. The effect of this on the poem is of course wholly in keeping with his claim for what Donne achieved. He purged the 'Muses garden'* of its pedantry, which grew there like a weed. The garden image of the first four lines is what became known as a Metaphysical 'conceit', a device intended to draw us into an active role as we read by taxing our imagination.

Carew is very aware of the way the unit of the couplet can lend itself to a pedantic tone if each statement is strictly, and all too neatly, wrapped up in pairs of rhyming lines. In reaction to this he draws his observations out over many lines. From the fourth line through to the end of the passage he uses a monetary conceit, which begins with the phrase 'Thou didst pay / The debts . . .' In so doing he effectively claims that Donne has responded to the appeal we saw Chapman making in the previous chapter; the English language is a vehicle fit for the greatest poetry:

* The Muses: Greek deities believed to preside over the arts of poetry, music and dance.

    . . . The subtle cheat
Of slie Exchanges, and the jugling feat
Of two-edg'd words, or whatsoever wrong
By ours was done the Greeke, or Latine tongue,
Thou hast redeem'd, and open'd Us a Mine
Or rich and pregnant phansie

    Once we have identified the conceit, we do indeed have the
pleasure of mining out the meaning. Greek and Latin are personi-
fied as devious, even dishonest financial dealers working at their
'slie Exchanges'. Poets have been short-changed in the past, but
Donne has 'redeem'd' them, meaning literally in financial
terminology 'paid off their debts'. In return we have now 'a
Mine / Of rich and pregnant phansie . . .'.

    Carew weaves his sense from line to line, giving us no rest; the
whole passage is effectively one long sentence, and we may be forgiven for not noticing the couplet structure in our attempt to
follow his argument. Carew's cavalier 'Metaphysical' treatment of
the couplet will become very clear if we compare his *Elegie* with
just four lines from a verse letter 'To A Lady' (written 1732–4) by
Alexander Pope (1688–1744):

  Men, some to Bus'ness, some to Pleasure take;
But ev'ry Woman is at heart a Rake:
Men, some to Quiet, some to public Strife;
But ev'ry Lady would be Queen for life.
    (*PAP*, p. 567 ll.215–18)

It must be immediately apparent how much more tightly controlled Pope's couplets are. Enjambment is relatively rare
throughout the poem. Pope represents a movement to return to a
more strictly orthodox ('Augustan') use of the form; though his
economy of words and the precision with which his point is made
hardly give us the impression of a poet who is controlled by, rather
than controlling, his chosen verse form. We should note also that
there is a larger pattern operating here than the couplet, acting
like an additional support for the poetic structure. The first and
third line exactly mirror each other in punctuation and syntax, as
do lines two and four. We might almost be lulled into believing
him by the sense of certainty generated by the verbal symmetry; or
is it pedantry?

The impression gained from reading sixteenth- and seventeenth-
century poetry is that, for all its variety, Thom Gunn's conviction

about the Elizabethans was broadly true of poetry certainly through to the latter half of the seventeenth century, and probably beyond. Art, and in particular poetry, was more central to the way the people to whom it was available thought, spoke, and behaved.

When we consider what is certainly one of the major poetic landmarks of the seventeenth century, John Milton's epic poem, *Paradise Lost*, we are given a further insight into the social climate which sustained this close relationship between the poet and society.

Paradise Lost is Milton's version of the biblical account of the fall of man and the promise of redemption. Its action spans the time between God's expulsion of Satan and the rebel angels from Heaven, and the expulsion of Adam and Eve from the Garden of Eden. Its religious theme indicates that if we are to understand anything of the readership for poetry in the period we are at present considering, we must recognize that religion was a real and potent factor in the way people thought and acted; religion and politics were at times virtually indistinguishable. Milton began work on *Paradise Lost* in 1658, just two years before the restoration of the Stuart monarchy in 1660. Prior to this England had been torn by civil war, the battle lines drawn between royalists and parliamentarians whose political beliefs were conceived of and expressed in religious terms.

Besides being a poet, Milton had become one of the principle pamphleteers of the Parliamentarian cause during these years. *Paradise Lost* was begun just as the great experiment of Oliver Cromwell's commonwealth was crumbling; through it Milton sought to express the sum total of his convictions at the highest, most complete level. In doing so he could assume, unlike Christian poets of our own time, that for the vast majority of his reading public, religion – specifically Christianity – was an integral part of their lives. In a society such as this, which accepted the concept of God as creator of the world, and as final arbiter of the destiny of men and nations, the attempt to express religious truths inevitably had a strong attraction for what were deemed the highest orders of literary and visual expression. At the same time, the forces of religious puritanism, growing steadily since the Reformation in the 1530s, were inclined to be increasingly suspicious of the tendency in art to celebrate worldly things, a love of life rather than of God. The society where such tensions could be artistically productive evidently had a very real and strong sense of the importance of spiritual values over material riches and rewards.

Recognizing the influence of this tension on sixteenth-, seventeenth- and eighteenth-century poetry is equally important for our reading of nineteenth- and twentieth-century poetry. Poets of the nineteenth century saw the waning of religious faith in their time as a genuinely portentous crisis that threatened the whole fabric of civilized society. Incorporated in this remorseless progress towards secularization was the loss of reverence for classical literature and tradition.

At its most pessimistic, this amounted to a sense of total decay, of the loss of a coherence and order for humanity that pointed towards impending anarchy. Just as coherence and order were marks of man's attainment of civilized life, so did poetry contribute to and depend upon the maintenance of the civilized virtues. The dramatic shifts in the religious and cultural consciousness of the late eighteenth and early nineteenth centuries were responsible on the one hand for terminating the assumed dominance of Christian ethics in society, while on the other they reflected a dramatic growth in population which, with the increase of literacy, made the survival of one dominant cultural model for art impossible.

Ever since the sixteenth century, the evolution of the English language has carried with it an implied challenge from northern European (otherwise known as 'Gothic') culture to the classical heritage of southern European, Italian culture. A growing and diversified public for literature in the eighteenth century was to realize that challenge, and the result was a proliferation of different literary modes.

From our vantage point in the late twentieth century, we may appreciate that these changes inevitably brought about the demise of poetry as it then was; the cultural disruption of the period was bound to disrupt the major vehicle of artistic expression born of and in part sustaining the passing order. New literary forms with the ability to adapt themselves in accordance with the changing times came in to fill the vacuum; in the nineteenth century this refers principally of course to the novel. The poet was left to redefine his art, a process which was to require the passage of many years, and arguably it still continues.

In the mean time poetry tended to be the art form through which individuals could do little more than lament the loss of a world in which their function in relation to their limited audience had been clearly understood. Milton, for example, saw *Paradise Lost* sell just 1,300 copies in two years, and his publisher had an agreement with him that no edition of his poem should exceed 1,500 copies. In a period when the literacy rate is believed to have been static (no significant movement coming until around 1780), this was no cause for concern. The privileged few who were likely to be reading poetry were also the privileged few in positions of power and influence in the country.

As we can appreciate from the extract from Wordsworth's sonnet used at the beginning of this chapter, Milton became one of the focal points for poets who were subsequently to suffer a crisis of confidence in their art. That sense of crisis was not infrequently expressed in language more or less derivative from *Paradise Lost*. During the eighteenth century, Miltonic epic became virtually the obligatory style for the poet intent on serious philosophical reflection, and it introduces us to a profoundly influential poetic form, that of blank verse.

In poetry, as in his theology, Milton was an innovator. He looked predictably enough to Italian Renaissance poetry for his models, but he chose a style which had yet to be established by Italian writers as wholly successful for the demands of the epic. Even the Italian poet Tasso (1544–95), whom Milton evidently revered, had failed to convince the literati of the day of the suitability of the form.

Blank verse offered the poet a degree of freedom far beyond anything we have seen in poetry up to this time. Rhyme, a sheet anchor of poetic control, always an effective means of heightening meaning when expertly used, was abandoned, as was any firm sense of the 'line' as necessarily a unit of expression (a tendency already there in Metaphysical poetry as we saw with Carew). What remained as a technical discipline was the iambic pentameter; for the rest, to avoid the effect of prose simply divided up into lines of equal length, the poet had to use language with great skill to create rhythmic patterns, and generally to lift the reader's imaginative response to the point where something of especial significance seemed to be being said.

Milton achieved this effect in part by his use of Latinate syntax or word order. The reader can understand what is written, but has to negotiate a slightly un-English, ornate phraseology; indeed, *Paradise Lost* reads at times like a literal translation from a Latin text. The subject of the poem itself, of course, gave him the opportunity to work up visual images of such magnitude and variety, that the form was brought to life in a way it has seldom been since. One example must suffice. The following lines are from Book IV (ll.172–93), and describe how Satan, arrived on Earth after an eventful journey from Hell, finally gains access to the Garden of Eden:

    Now to th'ascent of that steep savage Hill
Satan had journied on, pensive and slow;
But further way found none, so thick entwin'd,
As one continu'd brake, the undergrowth
Of shrubs and tangling bushes had perplext   5
All path of Man or Beast that past that way:
One Gate there onely was, and that look'd East
On th'other side: which when th'arch-fellon saw
Due entrance he disdaind, and in contempt,
At one slight bound high overleap'd all bound   10
Of Hill or highest Wall, and sheer within
Lights on his feet. As when a prowling Wolfe,
Whom hunger drives to seek new haunt for prey,
Watching where Shepherds pen thir Flocks at eeve
In hurdl'd Cotes amid the field secure,   15
Leaps o're the fence with ease into the Fould:
Or as a Thief bent to unhoord the cash
Of some rich Burgher, whose substantial dores,
Cross-barrd and bolted fast, fear no assault,
In at the window climbes, or o're the tiles;   20
So clomb this first grand Thief into God's Fould:
So since into his Church lewd Hirelings climbe.
    (*PJM*, pp. 620–1)

As ever, to begin to appreciate the poetry, we have to enter into
partnership with the writer. The drama and interest of this passage, especially on a first reading, will not become apparent unless
we actively seek it out.

    We should first consider the way Milton is using the iambic
pentameter line, for this is really the foundation upon which all
else is built. We must recognize that the beginning of each line
signifies a step forward through the narration, even as it clearly
defines our progress through the poem in physical terms on the
page. The meaning of what is written may be enhanced by that
potential moment of emphasis, or it may suppress it, in the latter
case creating an atmosphere of growing tension and expectancy.

    The emphasis is clearly suppressed in the first line, the word
'Now' serves only to hasten us on into the rest of the sentence. The
first line sets the scene ready for the main character of the moment
to make his dramatic entry, which he does at the beginning of line
two. Milton, like a public speaker wishing to capture his
audience's attention, withholds the subject of his sentence, thus
making all the more vivid what would otherwise be little more
than a vague backcloth.

    Now consider his manipulation of rhythm in the first two lines.
The iambic, approximating to normal speech rhythm, gives the

line its fundamental shape. It is disrupted by 'Satan', a word we tend to scan with equal if not long and short emphases (the trochee). We are redirected to iambics by the phrase which follows: 'hăd jóur.nĭed ón'. Then the remainder of the line breaks against the underlying rhythm. It is most naturally scanned 'long-short-short.long' (a 'dactyl trisyllable' followed by a 'spondee'), thus: 'pénsĭve ănd.slów'. The effect is to enact physically the sense of the passage, the line is slowed down. Compare this with the fluidity of line one: 'Nŏw tó.th̄'ascént.ŏf thát.stĕep sáv.ăge Híll'.

This, then, is Milton exploiting his chosen form to give us his meaning in every way open to him.

In the four lines which follow we are allowed no rest, the clause winds on as Satan's eye travels across an impenetrable wall 'of shrubs and tangling bushes'. The iambic rhythm is here undisturbed, the effect being therefore of a steady sweep of the eye across a wide vista.

The cumulative effect is one of the safety of God's treasured creation that lives beyond the forbidding barrier. Knowing as we do that Satan will eventually gain access, we expect at the very least a laborious penetration of the jungle. It is very much to Milton's purpose that he should now contradict the impression he has created. From a weary, perplexed traveller, Satan is suddenly transformed to become the dangerous enemy of mankind he truly is, the enemy we are often in danger of underestimating or even forgetting:

One Gate there onely was, and that look'd East
On th'other side: which when th'arch-fellon saw
Due entrance he disdained, and in contempt,
At one slight bound high overleap'd all bound
Of Hill or highest Wall, and sheer within
Lights on his feet.
    (ll.7–12 above)

Milton has carefully prepared us to imagine Satan wearily confused by the barrier and its one gate; the word 'perplext' (l.5) is used specifically to mislead us in this respect. His disdain and contempt come as a worrying surprise (l.9), and what follows would seem directly to challenge the confidence we have been encouraged to have in God's wisdom and power: 'At one slight bound high overleap'd all bound/Of Hill or highest Wall, and sheer within/Lights on his feet'. The words could not be chosen more carefully ('slight' and 'sheer', for example, give a wonderful sense of the ease with which Satan accomplishes his task); nor could the lines be more expressively arranged. With his repetition of the word 'bound' Milton requires us to consider its meaning with particular care. A 'slight bound' (meaning leap) by Satan negates every 'bound' (meaning moral restriction) that God has placed on Satan himself, and indeed on creation in general (or so it seems at this point in the narration).

After the wearisome effort of what has gone before, the swift ease of Satan's defiance of God is enacted by lines which eventually deposit Satan in Eden in just four smoothly scanned syllables, 'Lights ón.hĭs féet'. We're there almost before we realize it. It is a professional job too – notice that he lands on his feet!

The epic by definition tells of momentous events and heroic deeds, and epic poetry evolved the convention of 'epic similes', comparisons which would impress the reader with the grandeur of their subject (a different technique from the conceit). Scarcely an incident may pass in a true epic poem without some such epic simile being employed. In this passage we have two, both of which are in traditional form, but adapted by Milton to remind us that, heroic as Satan may seem, he is nevertheless evil. The wolf leaping into the sheepfold (ll.12–16), and the thief breaking into a rich man's house (ll.17–21) are graphically described and serve to bring the meaning into a contemporary context. Following the imagined scene of a vast, primeval wilderness outside the Garden of Eden, there is an engaging homeliness about the reference to a thief climbing in at the window, 'or o'er the tiles'.

Having brought us to his own time, Milton, poet of the Puritan party, takes the opportunity to administer a swift slap in the face to the Established Church and its worldly ministers: 'So since into his Church lewd Hirelings climbe'. 'Hirelings' refers to men prepared to hire themselves out to the ministry for the money they might make, rather than through a sense of religious vocation.

The possibilities of this passage have by no means been exhausted. *Paradise Lost* is remarkable for its intensity; we can see how Milton is always at work, every image, every word is carefully chosen. Nothing happens at random. The poem seems to demand an investigation rather than a 'reading', and it is no less a poem for that fact. The reader, as I hope has already become apparent, has a genuinely creative part to play in realizing the poetry. Finding – or 'reading in' – meaning is required of us and should not, as is sadly often the case, be viewed with suspicion. We should always be prepared, of course, to recognize 'our' *Paradise Lost* as one among many versions, all of which will be likely to reveal new possibilities for the text.

Paradise Lost is a huge poem; it is divided into twelve Books, each Book consisting of seven hundred or so lines of blank verse arranged in paragraph form. In terms of size alone, therefore, it is a literary phenomenon which – loved or hated – cannot be ignored. But size alone does not explain why it subsequently dominated the writing of poetry in the way it did, and indeed why it still has a lasting influence. The answer lies initially with the historical significance of the English Civil War. While many details relating to the war are still hotly debated, there is no doubt that it marked a traumatic period of social and political dislocation in the mid seventeenth century. *Paradise Lost* emerges from the confusion of a society undergoing fundamental processes of change, and stands as the monumental culmination of English Renaissance culture. It is a Latinate epic poem, into which Milton poured the entire range of literary reference available to a scholar not just of the classical world, but of Northern European traditions also; not just of Christianity, but of Judaism and a whole array of other religions and cults then being researched. The enquiring spirit of an emerging nation in the sixteenth century is synthesized, and fed into a poetic project which in scale and intent would seem to rival the Bible itself; and there is more, for as we have seen, it was a project which in the last resort turned against the society which had made it possible. Milton attacked an establishment he saw as having become corrupt and spiritually barren. It is the wave which at its highest point is already beginning to break and disperse.

As the culmination of a cultural tradition which subsequently slid into decline, a cultural tradition which had elevated poetry through Milton's mastery of the epic form to a virtually unassailable dominance over all other literary forms, *Paradise Lost* understandably became a central point of reference in respect of its language, its blank verse technique, and its epic simile convention for poets who would subsequently strive to recapture the exalted position Milton had won for himself as poet, philosopher and political orator. *Paradise Lost* took its place alongside Cranmer's Prayer Book of 1549 and the King James Bible of 1611 as a major guide to what language should sound like at its most influential and serious level: in other words, at its most 'poetic'.

Evidence of the hold *Paradise Lost* retained over the poetic imagination during the period of cultural crisis in the late eighteenth and early nineteenth centuries is easily found. Milton was a repeated point of reference for all the major Romantic poets. If, like Shelley, they rejected his brand of religion, they remained prepared to acknowledge the magnitude of his achievement. William Blake and William Wordsworth were probably the two Romantic poets most deeply influenced by Milton's work, more so even than John Keats.

Wordsworth became convinced that he had a vocation to write a philosophical poem of epic proportions. Its purpose was to reconcile his generation to the collapse of the humanitarian, political ideals encouraged by the outbreak of the French Revolution in 1789. The hope that a new era of liberty was dawning was crushed first by the unforseen violent radicalism of the revolution, then by its imperialist aftermath under Napoleon.

The Recluse, as the poem was to be called, was, like *Paradise Lost*, to rise from the ashes of revolutionary failure. By way of preparation for this task, Wordsworth found it necessary to compile an account of his own life, a poem which has become known as *The Prelude*. The form it took should be familiar enough to us now, through our reading of Milton:

As one who hangs down-bending from the side
Of a slow-moving boat, upon the breast
Of a still water, solacing himself
With such discoveries as his eye can make
Beneath him in the bottom of the deep,   5
Sees many beauteous sights – weeds, fishes, flowers,
Grots, pebbles, roots of trees, and fancies more,
Yet often is perplexed and cannot part
The shadow from the substance, rocks and sky,
Mountains and clouds, reflected in the depth   10
Of the clear flood, from things which there abide
In their true dwelling; now is crossed by gleam
Of his own image, by a sunbeam now,
And wavering motions sent he knows not whence,
Impediments that make his task more sweet;   15
Such pleasant office have we long pursued
Incumbent o'er the surface of past time
With like success, nor often have appeared
Shapes fairer or less doubtfully discerned
Than these to which the Tale, indulgent Friend!   20
Would now direct thy notice
(*WPW*, p. 518, Book IV, ll.256–76)

The Prelude, which ran eventually to 14 Books, is in blank verse employing the techniques worked out by Milton: enjambment, rhythmic variations from the basic iambic, carefully chosen, often alliterative words. Here in particular we have Wordsworth's version of the epic simile. It is signalled by the opening words, 'As one . . .', reminiscent of Milton's use of 'As when' for the similes from *Paradise Lost* quoted above, and echoing precisely his manner elsewhere; at the beginning of Book XII, for example:

As one who in his journey bates at Noone,
Though bent on speed, so heer the Arch-angel paus'd

If we re-read the Milton passage and turn again to Wordsworth's *Prelude*, we find it differs in being less muscle-bound, less intense, though no less self-conscious in its use of language. The purpose of the simile is to investigate the idea of reflection: literally reflections seen on a lake surface made complex by their merging with what is seen beneath the surface ('and cannot part/The shadow from the substance' ll.8–9); and reflection as a description of his own poetic act, reflecting on his past ('o'er the surface of past time' l.17), where the remembered past is coloured by present experience.

The poet himself is central to the poem in a way Milton never was to *Paradise Lost*, in addition to which the *substance* of Wordsworth's simile, the natural objects he so carefully numbers, 'weeds, fishes, flowers,/Grots, pebbles, roots of trees', assume an importance in their own right; they are not the generalized references we find Milton using. 'Nature' is present in *Paradise Lost* only as a background (albeit strikingly portrayed, as at the beginning of the passage discussed above), certainly it is never there for its own sake. Wordsworth, in the early years of the nineteenth century, could not assume – as Milton could – that his readership would recognize the centrality of a Christian theme, supported by references to classical mythology. A common language for this kind of poetry has gone. Wordsworth's audience for *The Prelude* is essentially an audience of one, himself. He attempts to escape from this unhealthy situation by bringing to bear the epic form established by the earlier poet. The intensely personal thus becomes clothed in the formal language of universally applicable poetry.

We have noted Wordsworth's use of a Miltonic opening for his simile; in addition to this we have the syntax of phrases like 'down-bending', 'Yet often is perplexed', 'wavering motions sent he knows not whence', which signify Miltonic poeticizing. In particular, the tone adopted in the last five lines assumes an air of authority bordering on pomposity, 'Such pleasant office have we long pursued . . .', which reminds us of Milton at his most pontifical: 'For Heav'nly minds from such distempers foule/Are ever clear' (*PJM*, p. 615, IV, ll.118–19). Note the characteristic inver-

sion of 'distempers foule', and how it is picked up in
Wordsworth's 'down-bending' and 'often is'.

The *Recluse* was intended to realize more completely the function of Miltonic epic. This point is made abundantly clear in an
extract from an unfinished section of that poem printed in his
'preface' to the one and only part of *The Recluse* he ever properly
completed, called *The Excursion*:

'On Man, on Nature, and on Human Life,
Musing in solitude, I oft perceive
Fair trains of imagery before me rise,
Accompanied by feelings of delight
Pure, or with no unpleasing sadness mixed,   5
And I am conscious of affecting throughts
And dear remembrances, whose presence soothes
Or elevates the Mind, intent to weigh
The good and evil of our mortal state.
  – To these emotions, whenceso'er they come,   10
Whether from breath of outward circumstance,
Or from the Soul – an impulse to herself –
I would give utterance in numerous verse.
Of Truth, of Grandeur, Beauty, Love, and Hope,
And melancholy Fear subdued by Faith;   15
Of blessed consolations in distress;
Of moral strength, and intellectual Power;
Of joy in widest commonalty spread;
Of the individual Mind that keeps her own
Inviolate retirement, subject there   20
To Conscience only, and the law supreme
Of that Intelligence which governs all –
I sing: – 'fit audience let me find though few!'
    (*WPW*, p. 590, ll.1–23)

To a reader for whom Wordsworth is the simple 'daffodil poet',
the poet of 'Nature', a passage such as this may well come as
something of a shock; yet it is his personal manifesto, and it is
unmistakably Miltonic. Compare it with an extract from the
opening paragraph of *Paradise Lost*:

Of Mans First Disobedience, and the Fruit
Of that Forbidden Tree, whose mortal taste
Brought Death into the World, and all our woe,
With loss of *Eden*, till one greater Man
Restore us, and regain the blissful Seat,
Sing Heav'nly Muse . . .
 . . . .
  . . . What in me is dark

Illumin, what is low raise and support;
That to the highth of this great Argument
I may assert Eternal Providence,
And justifie the wayes of God to men.

Both poets have what Milton calls a 'great Argument', and clearly Wordsworth's is not – because it can no longer be – as single-mindedly 'religious' as that of the seventeenth-century poet. Yet the Miltonic grandeur of language and phrase claim an equivalent status, to the point where he actually quotes *Paradise Lost* ('fit audience let me find though few') without any disturbance of his own rhetoric.*

Milton's own use of that phrase was to explain that all he required for his poem was a suitably select audience. In Wordsworth's case, we are reminded of his anxiety about finding a readership; the immediacy of Milton's Christian theme may no longer be assumed. He must, as he says, 'breathe in worlds / To which the heaven of heavens is but a veil' (ll.29–30). The 'region' (l.41), by which he means subject, of his poem is thus different, but to describe what that region is, he uses the classical simile technique learned from Milton:

. . . Not Chaos, not
The darkest pit of lowest Erebus,
Nor aught of blinder vacancy, scooped out
By help of dreams – can breed such fear and awe
As fall upon us often when we look
Into our Minds, into the Mind of Man –
My haunt, and the main region of my song.
    (*WPW*, p. 590, ll.35–41)

The negative construction brings to mind Milton's description of the figure of Sin, encountered by Satan in Book II of *Paradise Lost*:

Farr less abhorred then these
Vex'd *Scylla* bathing in the Sea that parts
Calabria from the hoarce *Trinacrian* shore:
Nor uglier follow the Night-Hag, when call'd
In secret, riding through the Air she comes
Lur'd with the smell of infant blood, to dance
With *Lapland* Witches, while the labouring Moon
Eclipses at their charms
    (*PJM*, pp. 539–40, ll.659–66)

---

* The quotation, slightly augmented by Wordsworth, is from *Paradise Lost* Book VII, l.23, and originally reads: '. . . fit audience find, though few'.

Wordsworth's invocation of Milton's epic style serves to emphasize the way the later poet saw himself as an isolated poet, addressing a readership (not unlike ourselves, perhaps) no longer equipped to understand poetry requiring familiarity with Christian theology and classical mythology:

```
        . . . by words
Which speak of nothing more than what we are,
Would I arouse the sensual from their sleep
Of Death, and win the vacant and the vain
To noble raptures
        (WPW, p. 590, ll.58–62)
```

Milton's audience was gone. *The Recluse* was designed not to reinstate that audience, but to educate a post French Revolution generation to receive once more *en masse* a poetry of universal significance, a poetry 'whose presence soothes/Or elevates the Mind, intent to weigh/The good and evil of our mortal state'.

It is all too easy for us now to reflect on how completely Wordsworth had misjudged what was happening in the literary world. He was writing at a time when, compared with the 1,300 copies of *Paradise Lost* sold over two years in a country whose population was approaching five and a half million, Walter Scott sold 6,000 copies of his first novel, *Waverley,* in six months, and Byron's romantic narrative poem, *The Corsair,* sold 10,000 copies on publication day. By contrast, the first edition of *The Excursion* ran to five hundred copies, it was published in 1814 (the same year as *Waverley* and *The Corsair*), and in the space of nine months just three hundred copies were sold. The total population of the country had by this time risen to around nine million, and over the next hundred years it would increase at a phenomenal rate to thirty-two and a half million. The reading public had already expanded during the eighteenth century to include a significant proportion of women, while in the nineteenth century the rapidly growing readership embraced an ever widening range of social classes; it was no longer essentially metropolitan; nor was it only the wealthy, privileged few who could afford to buy books. Wordsworth lived to see Dickens selling 50,000 copies of the first number of *Nicholas Nickleby*, 30,000 to 40,000 of *The Cricket on the Hearth*, and 30,000 of the first issue of *Dombey and Son*. It was another world from the one in which Wordsworth had grown up, one where the neo-Miltonic role of the poet as envisaged in *The Recluse* could never be realized.

Perhaps the best known expression of the conviction that such a retrieval of the poet's role was impossible came from Matthew Arnold, when in 1867 he published *Dover Beach*. For Arnold the old faiths upon which civilization (and poetry) depended were lost for ever:

The sea is calm to-night.
The tide is full, the moon lies fair
Upon the straits;- on the French coast the light
Gleams and is gone; the cliffs of England stand,
Glimmering and vast, out in the tranquil bay.   5
Come to the window, sweet is the night-air!
Only, from the long line of spray
Where the sea meets the moon-blanch'd land,
Listen! You hear the grating roar
Of pebbles which the waves draw back, and fling,   10
At their return, up the high strand,
Begin, and cease, and then again begin,
With tremulous cadence slow, and bring
The eternal note of sadness in.

Sophocles long ago   15
Heard it on the Agean, and it brought
Into his mind the turbid ebb and flow
Of human misery; we
Find also in the sound a thought,
Hearing it by this distant northern sea.   20

The Sea of Faith
Was once, too, at the full, and round earth's shore
Lay like the folds of a bright girdle furl'd.
But now I only hear
Its melancholy, long, withdrawing roar,   25
Retreating, to the breath
Of the night wind, down the vast edges drear
And naked shingles of the world.

Ah, love, let us be true
To one another! for the world, which seems   30
To lie before us like a land of dreams,
So various, so beautiful, so new,
Hath really neither joy, nor love, nor light,
Nor certitude, nor peace, nor help for pain;
And we are here as on a darkling plain   35
Swept with confused alarms of struggle and flight,
Where ignorant armies clash by night.
          (*PFD*, pp. 49–50)

There is nothing left to be 'Miltonic' about, and the Miltonic structure is abandoned. We have instead an underpinning of these lines of uneven length with irregular rhyme, an echo of the style of the Greek poet Pindar (*c*.522–442 BC). Arnold, excluded from any social identity beyond that which he can establish through isolated relationships (ll.29–34), has become sole arbiter of the extent of his stanzas and lines. Miltonic touches of syntax ('With tremulous cadence slow', l.13), his use of iambics and references to the classical world (ll.15–20), all pay tribute to a tone of high seriousness of the past, not the present.

Technically, of course, *Dover Beach* is a superbly conceived poem; Arnold's sense of the physical effect of the lines gives the poem great emotional impact. *Dover Beach* is accompanied by the constant but irregular sound of waves breaking on the shore, and the lines come and go in uneven surges, giving a faltering momentum to the argument.

Following Wordsworth and *The Recluse*, it is Tennyson who in the nineteenth century set out to achieve epic status in traditional form with his Arthurian *Idylls of the King* (published between 1859 and 1885). The subjects of *The Recluse* and *Idylls* differ significantly. Wordsworth's one published section of his poem, *The Excursion*, had as its basic narrative the story of a man fired with hope by the idealism of the French Revolution in its infancy. He is reduced to despair (a crucial ingredient of which is his loss of religious faith) by the inhumanity surrounding subsequent events. He is gradually brought within sight of redemption in the course of the poem by a series of arguments and moral tales meted out over nine Books, most of which run to over a thousand lines apiece. This is not the traditional subject-matter of epic; but where the subject-matter of *Paradise Lost* was clearly of immediate relevance to the poet's own time given the centrality of religious conflict in the Civil War period, Wordsworth was in like manner addressing his poem to matters of the deepest significance for the post-war generation of the Napoleonic era, even if he had chosen 'unknowns' to act out his drama rather than heroes long established through Christian and classical culture.

Tennyson's choice of Arthurian mythology was in one respect a return to orthodox epic convention; but in so doing he was concurring with Arnold's conviction that here was a cause that had already been fought and irretrievably lost. As the major poet of the day, therefore, he produced a major work of poetry which paradoxically confirmed the practise of poetry as anachronistic, and with it blank verse as the language of a lost cause. Any poet who sought an alternative form ran the risk of being thought less than serious, yet a poet writing in the inflated language and form traditionally associated with blank verse was patently in retreat from the modern world. All the frustrations of this situation come together in Tristram's despairing monologue as he sees the fellowship of the Round Table collapsing through intrigue and corruption:

Then Tristram, pacing moodily up and down,
'Vows! did you keep the vow you made to Mark
More than I mine? Lied, say ye? Nay, but learnt,
The vow that binds too strictly snaps itself –
My knighthood taught me this – ay, being snapt –
We run more counter to the soul thereof
Than we had never sworn. I swear no more.
I swore to the great King, and am forsworn.
For once – ev'n to the height – I honour'd him.
"Man, is he man at all?" methought, when first
I rode from our rough Lyonesse, and beheld
The victor of the pagan throned in hall –
His hair, a sun that ray'd from off a brow
Like hillsnow high in heaven, the steel-blue eyes,
The golden beard that clothed his lips with light –
Moreover, that weird legend of his birth,
With Merlin's mystic babble about his end
Amazed me; then, his foot was on a stool
Shaped as a dragon; he seem'd to me no man,
But Michael trampling Satan; so I swear,
Being amazed: but this went by – The vows!
O ay – the wholesome madness of an hour –
They served their use, their time; for every knight
Believed himself a greater than himself,
And every follower eyed him as a God;
Till he, being lifted up beyond himself,
Did mightier deeds than elsewhere he had done,
And so the realm was made; but then their vows –
First mainly thro' that sullying of our Queen –
Began to gall the knighthood, asking whence
Had Arthur right to bind them to himself?'
(*Idylls of the King*, 'The Last Tournament', pp. 265–6, ll.649–79)

The desperate energy which Tennyson injects into these lines, driving on rhythmically and grammatically from line to line, 'We run more counter to the soul thereof/Than we had never sworn . . .', then halting the flow with shorter, broken exclamations, 'Than we had never sworn. I swear no more', shows a masterful adaptation of the form; but tells at the same time of its demise. The theme, ultimately, is one with which we are now all too familiar, the loss of social coherence, and with it the loss of the knights' – and the poets' – role.

4
READING MODERN POETRY: TRADITION AND INNOVATION

Malt does more than Milton can
To justify God's ways to man.

(Housman, 1859–1936, *A Shropshire Lad*, lxii)

The impact of Miltonic blank verse on English poetry has been described as primarily a negative influence. When we consider Milton's eighteenth-century disciples and their offerings (James Thomson's *Liberty* (1734–6), Edward Young's *Night Thoughts* (1742–5), Robert Blair's *The Grave* (1743), Mark Akenside's *The Pleasures of Imagination* (1744)), negative may indeed seem to be a charitable description; though that is not to say the poems mentioned are entirely without merit, they certainly attracted a good deal of interest in their own time.

Blank verse, however, was far from enjoying a monopoly over poetic form from the mid seventeenth century on. Other traditional, classical verse forms persisted for use in satirical, descriptive, narrative or sentimental poetry. Of these, probably the most persistent was the rhyming couplet. Here is John Dryden's satirical portrait of the Earl of Shaftesbury, written in 1681. The grandeur of Milton's blank verse, with its long phrases and extended similies, is gone. Dryden's use of the rhyming couplet creates a powerfully energetic driving force for his poetry, which counteracts a style of language tending towards epigrammatic brevity:

Great Wits are sure to Madness near alli'd;
And thin Partitions do their Bounds divide:
Else, why should he, with Wealth and Honour blest,
Refuse his Age the needful hours of Rest?
Punish a Body which he coud not please,
Bankrupt of Life, yet Prodigal of Ease?
And all to leave, what with his Toil he won,

To that unfeather'd, two-legg'd thing, a Son:
Got, while his Soul did Huddled Notions trie;
And born a shapeless Lump, like Anarchy.
    (*Absalom and Achitophel*, ll.163–72)

The appeal of the rhyming couplet lay to a large degree in its versatility. In the latter half of the eighteenth century, with Dryden (1631–1700) and Pope still popular, and with Dr Johnson still alive and defending classical 'Augustan' literary forms against 'Gothic' intrusions, it was possible for Oliver Goldsmith (1730–74) to use couplets for a poem that could hardly have been more different from *Absalom and Achitophel*. *The Deserted Village* (1770) is a sentimental lament for a lost golden age of pastoral simplicity. At a first reading we might be forgiven for seeing no stylistic connection at all between this and the wit of Dryden or Pope:

In all my wanderings round this world of care,
In all my griefs – and God has given my share –
I still had hopes my latest hours to crown,
Amidst these humble bowers to lay me down;
To husband out life's taper at the close,
And keep the flame from wasting by repose.
I still had hopes, for pride attends us still,
Amidst the swains to show my book-learn'd skill,
Around my fire an evening group to draw,
And tell of all I felt, and all I saw;
And as an hare, whom hounds and horns pursue,
Pants to the place from whence at first she flew,
I still had hopes, my long vexations pass'd,
Here to return – and die at home at last.
    (*TLA*, p. 56, ll.83–96)

The Deserted Village has often been analysed to reveal the increasing sense of isolation that poets of this period were experiencing, and this passage could well be used to support that interpretation. While Dryden is generally thought of as a 'professional' poet, a man who lived as a journalist, writing his poetry in the market place, Goldsmith portrays himself as cut off from his roots, wandering in 'this world of care', returning to his native village only to find it deserted, his 'public' vanished: 'I still had hopes, for pride attends us still, / Amidst the swains to show my book-learn'd skill'.

Poetry during the eighteenth century is often described as losing its sense of direction after Pope, and drifting into a state of limbo. There is certainly plenty of evidence to support this view, and it was partly a reaction to the fallen status of the art that encouraged the early Romantics to begin experimenting anew with poetic form (in the year *The Deserted Village* was published Blake was thirteen and Wordsworth was literally making his entry into the world). This meant reinvestigating less fashionable forms – the sonnet and the Spenserian stanza were to a degree reinstated – and seeking to reanimate well worn classical conventions. The ode, a classical form not yet mentioned, became particularly popular. Originally the ode was a poem of some complexity intended to be sung. It emerged now loosely interpreted as a poem on an exalted subject consisting of rhymed verses which could be of varying length; nor need there be any consistency within the verses of line length. It possessed, in other words, the flexibility that a new generation of poets wishing to distance themselves from academic classicism sought.

John Keats wrote probably the best known odes of the Romantic period. If we turn from Keats, however, to Wordsworth's *Ode: Intimations of Immortality*, to Coleridge's *Ode: Dejection*, or to Shelley's *Ode to the West Wind*, we will find each of these poems varying considerably in form, each a revelation of the poet's own personality. The Romantic poet is asserting his authority over the form, not vice versa.

This constitutes a reaction against the drift of Goldsmith's poetry, which threatened to write the poet into oblivion. For the poet to rediscover himself he had also to rediscover his public. To this end poets of this period began to show increasing interest in so-called ballad form. It was no new thing, but in a century when for the first time attempts were being made to formulate a literary history of England,* the ballad emerged as a form that had existed in this country prior to the introduction of European, classical styles, and one moreover which had spoken directly to ordinary people in their own language. Through an increasingly inflexible attitude to classical form, the contemporary poet had lost touch with the far from static state of the reading public. In the short, regularly scanned and rhymed verses of the ballad narrative lay a potential key to recapturing their attention. This is what Wordsworth and Coleridge aimed to do in *Lyrical Ballads*.†

---

* Thomas Warton (1728–90), *History of English Poetry* (pub. 1774–81). Warton played a leading part in re-establishing sonnet form, and in encouraging renewed interest in Spenser.

† First published 1798, a second edition in 1800 with additional poems and an extended 'preface' (quoted in Chapter 2, pp. 12–13).

The content was to remain serious and thought-provoking, the form was to be innovatory.

Coleridge's *The Rime of the Ancient Mariner* remains one of the best known Romantic ballad poems; it was the first poem a reader of *Lyrical Ballads* turned to. In part it is pastiche, written to imitate the style and tone of the ancient ballads that were then so popular, yet at the same time it incorporated haunting themes of sacrifice and atonement that have fascinated readers ever since:

It is an ancient Mariner,
And he stoppeth one of three.
'By thy long grey beard and glittering eye,
Now wherefore stopp'st thou me?

'The Bridegroom's doors are opened wide,
And I am next of kin;
The guests are met, the feast is set:
May'st hear the merry din.'

He holds him with his skinny hand,
'There was ship,' quoth he.
'Hold off! unhand me, grey-beard loon!'
Eftsoons his hand dropt he.

He holds him with his glittering eye –
The Wedding-Guest stood still,
And listens like a three years' child:
The Mariner hath his will.
    (*PBRV*, pp. 155–6, stanzas i–iv)

In the light of what has previously been said, it is interesting to be reminded that the first poem in *Lyrical Ballads* begins with this powerful description of the narrator having to struggle desperately to secure his audience.

The contrast with the formality of classical poetry is obvious; the hypnotic power of the Mariner is embodied in the hypnotic, chant-like quality of the verse, and the verse tells a story of universal appeal, of a ship lost at sea and of the weird experiences of the sole surviving member of the crew.

Ballad form has continued to attract poets on into the twentieth century; for the modern poet it is a conveniently versatile medium, by no means thought of as necessarily requiring the rhythmic predictability evident in Coleridge's *Ancient Mariner*.

Gerard Manley Hopkins (1844–89), writing at the end of the nineteenth century, was able to sustain a ballad structure – with all its tendencies to predictability – without sacrificing his determination to be stylistically innovative. He

evidently felt that where his poems drew on public events rather
than personal experiences, the traditionally 'public' form of the
ballad was the correct one to use. The following extract from *The
Loss of the Eurydice* illustrates this well:

The Eurydice – it concerned thee, O Lord:
Three hundred souls, O alas! on board,
   Some asleep unawakened, all un-
warned, eleven fathoms fallen

Where she foundered! One stroke   5
Felled and furled them, the hearts of oak!
   And flockbells off the aerial
Downs' forefalls beat to the burial.

For did she pride her, freighted fully, on
Bounden bales or a hoard of bullion? –   10
   Precious passing measure,
Lads and men her lade and treasure.

She had come from a cruise, training seamen –
Men, boldboys soon to be men:
   Must it, worst weather,   15
Blast bole and bloom together?

No Atlantic squall overwrought her
Or rearing billow of the Biscay water:
   Home was hard at hand
And the blow bore from the land.   20

And you were a liar, O blue March day.
Bright sun lanced fire in the heavenly bay;
   But what black Boreas wrecked her? he
Came equipped, deadly-electric,

A beetling baldbright cloud thorough England   25
Riding: there did storms not mingle? and
   Hailropes hustle and grind their
Heavengravel? wolfsnow, worlds of it, wind there?

Now Carisbrook Keep goes under in gloom;
Now it overvaults Appledurcombe;
   Now near by Ventnor town
It hurls, hurls off Boniface Down.

Too proud, too proud, what a press she bore!
Royal, and all her royals wore.
   Sharp with her, shorten sail!
Too late; lost; gone with the gale.   35
   (*GMH*, pp. 33–4)

Hopkins put word order, and indeed word coinage ('Hailropes', 'Heavengravel') completely at the mercy of intensification of meaning, to which end he also introduced a powerful technique of alliteration; in verse two, for example, we have 'foundered . . . Felled and furled . . . flockbells . . . forefalls', and the final, sombre 'beat to the burial.' The effect of this is to combine a sense of often startling originality with a reversion to the poetic techniques of early English poetry, the 'Gothic' style which had fascinated Edmund Spenser in the sixteenth century. Verse seven is a particularly good example of the way Hopkins manipulates and moulds language and syntax; the 'verse', however, is by no means an enclosed unit of sense in this poem, and it is necessary to quote from the last two lines of the previous verse:

But what black Boreas wrecked her? he
Came equipped, deadly-electric,

A beetling baldbright cloud thorough England
Riding: there did storms not mingle? and
    Hailropes hustle and grind their
Heavengravel? wolfsnow, worlds of it, wind there?

The sense we have that this verse is constructed according to a regular, predictable pattern arises in the first instance from its similarity in typographic appearance to all the other verses in the poem. Having established an important *visual* link with the traditional ballad form, Hopkins proceeds to make it his own by incorporating the rhythmic and syntactical experimentation for which his poetry became famous. We might scan the first line of verse seven: 'A béetling báldbright clóud thorough Eńgland', but any attempt at scansion of the poem as a whole reveals a continual, restless shifting of stresses. The first line of the second verse, for example, suggests the following: 'Whére she foúndered! Ońe stróke . . .' And yet the hypnotic quality of *The Ancient Mariner*, the sense of a regular beat beyond the irregularities, exists for the poem as a whole.

Rhyme is a key factor here, confirming line endings regardless of the syllabic and rhythmic variety achieved through Hopkins's use of 'sprung rhythm'. But in the first verse we can see how the poet – unlike Coleridge – was prepared even to investigate and challenge the orthodox matter of a line ending in order to intensify meaning:

Some asleep unawakened, all un-
warned, eleven fathoms fallen

The two lines are made to turn on the word 'un/warned', and that
word, made unfamiliar by the poetic device of the 'line' of verse
ending at the point it does, signifies that it is not to be thought of
as simply emphasizing the sense of 'unawakened'. For Hopkins, a
profoundly religious man, to be prepared for one's death was
crucial.

The function of *The Loss of the Eurydice* at its most basic is to
rehearse publicly the story of the tragedy of 1878, to imprint the
event on our consciousness 'lest we forget'; in his view those that
perished were people for whom we must pray.

In the twentieth century, ballad form has often been adopted
by poets who wish to satirize aspects of their society. Charles
Causley (b.1917) is one of our most successful contemporary bal-
ladeers, and his poem, *My Friend Maloney*, with its uneven scansion held doggedly in place by rhyme and line, is an excellent
example of the continuing attraction of the form (see *BP*
pp. 118–19). Another twentieth-century poet who has used the
form to great effect is W.H. Auden, 'As I walked out one evening' is one of his best known ballad poems.

Poetic forms established within the social and cultural context
of the sixteenth and seventeenth centuries have of course always
had the power to attract poets to them, and our understanding of
the Romantic Movement would be seriously incomplete without a
recognition of Shelley's avid classicism, Keat's fascination with
classical art forms, and – in their own different ways – both
Wordsworth's and Byron's life-long admiration of the poetry of
Pope.

Despite this, the major trend in poetry since the Romantics, has
been to challenge the dominance of formal rules of presentation.
One way of explaining this would be to say that, with the passing
of a coherent social and religious environment, poets have been
left to search for their audience among many audiences, unsure of
what their cultural wave-length might be; unsure, even, as to
whether there is a cultural wave-length available for their particular art.

The major stylistic poetic development to emerge from this situation has been 'free verse' (otherwise called *vers libre*). Milton, it
could be argued, was at least in part as responsible for the arrival
of free verse as he was for blighting so many English poets of the

eighteenth and nineteenth centuries with the conviction that 'serious', or 'great' poetry was inseparable from blank verse. Milton's choice of form for his epic was a challenge to English classical orthodoxy, just as his political position placed him at odds with the establishment. The effect of his choice of blank verse was one of liberation from the considerable control imposed – from without, as it were – by the rhyming couplet unit. Blank verse was a significant step towards handing over full control to the poet, who became responsible for whatever linguistic disciplines might be needed. In Milton's case, of course, it remained highly disciplined.

We have already seen from Wordsworth's *Prelude*, how in the early nineteenth century, the underlying metrical precision of *Paradise Lost* could be relaxed if the poet wished it, producing poetry of a reflective, meditative quality quite distinct from its Miltonic model. It was in the logic of the Romantic Movement, with its restless challenging of authority and tradition, its sensitivity to contemporary debates on individual freedom within society, its love of variety and its reassertion of spiritual energy over the tyranny of eighteenth-century rationalism, that externally imposed rules for the poet should be steadily eroded.

In the Romantic period itself, only William Blake actually went so far as to write in free verse, and then only in one section (the 'Argument') of a work written in prose, *The Marriage of Heaven and Hell* (*c.*1793). Blake was here something in the order of a hundred years before his time. Victorian poets, as even our brief survey will have indicated, were not to follow his lead, fascinated as some of them were by his writing. Walt Whitman (1819–92) writing in America, along with the French *vers libre* poets in the latter part of the nineteenth century, were largely responsible for revealing the possibilities of free verse to a later generation of English poets. During the nineteenth century in England, it was arguably the novel, becoming increasingly the dominant literary mode, which annexed and developed the poetic qualities of language in the liberated manner of free verse. We have already had an example of this from Dickens's *Dombey and Son* quoted in Chapter 1.

Mention of Whitman at this point signifies the beginning of a new and important development not just for English poetry, but for the arts in general. The influence of America on our cultural life during the twentieth century is everywhere obvious, and in poetry has manifested itself as a challenge to our otherwise insular tendency to abide by the traditional verse forms established in previous centuries. Some consideration therefore – however brief – of American poetry since Whitman's time is necessary, particularly as it relates directly to the introduction and development of techniques in free verse.

In America, Whitman was a poet who remained largely unread in his own life-time. Set against his nineteenth-century contemporaries, Emerson (1803–82), Longfellow (1807–82), Whittier (1807–92) and Lowell (1819–91), he appears profoundly unorthodox, writing with scant regard for the metrical models established by English poetry, and with no interest whatever in the demands of the English reading public. From one of his shorter poems, *The Dalliance of Eagles*, we can begin to appreciate an originality in his free verse style that would genuinely have startled a transatlantic reader of Tennyson, Arnold or Browning:

Skirting the river road, (my forenoon walk, my rest,)
Skyward in air a sudden muffled sound, the dalliance of eagles,
The rushing amorous contact high in space together,
The clinching interlocking claws, a living, fierce, gyrating wheel,
Four beating wings, two beaks, a swirling mass tight grappling,
In tumbling turning, clustering loops, straight downward falling,
Till o'er the river pois'd, the twain yet one, a moment's lull,
A motionless still balance in the air, then parting, talons loosing,
Upward again on slow-firm pinions slanting, their separate diverse
    flight,
She hers, he his, pursuing.
    (*AP*, p. 60)

The sense of immediacy which is such an important part of this poem is achieved initially through the brevity of his introduction. In his haste Whitman is prepared to omit all but the essential words, thus 'Skyward in the air' becomes 'Skyward in air . . .'. Then from line three we have the constant use of present participles, 'rushing', 'clinching interlocking', '. . . a swirling mass tight grappling'. The action is taking place at the moment of narration, leaving no time for reflection, no time to get a clear picture of what is happening. The pace of the first six lines of the poem is the consequence of bringing together words with intensity implicit in their meaning, often acquiring emphasis from their sound: 'In tumbling turning, clustering loops, straight downward falling'. We should note here also the rearrangement of the final three words. 'Falling straight downward' might be syntactically more normal, but poetically the meaning is dramatized by leaving the most important word until last, a technique which ensures that 'falling' will be stressed.

The tempo is slowed in the following line by its division into three more or less evenly spaced phrases, while words such as 'pois'd', 'motionless' and the compound 'slow-firm' contribute to the effect, as does the long ninth line with its intentionally tautological use of 'separate diverse', bringing the movement of sense to a standstill. The final, brief line, comes as an unsentimental account of the reinstatement of the eagles' separateness after mating.

No matter where one looks among Whitman's contemporaries, the contrast can hardly fail to be striking. John Whittier, for example, wrote about nature in a very different way. Where Whitman's relation of an incident in the American wilderness is designed to startle us (and may well also have shocked a nineteenth-century reader), Whittier offers a traditionally reflective view of a far tamer landscape in *Telling the Bees*:

Here is the place; right over the hill
  Runs the path I took;
You can see the gap in the old wall still,
  And the stepping-stones in the shallow brook.

There is the house, with the gate red-barred,
  And the poplars tall;
And the barn's brown length, and the cattle-yard,
  And the white horns tossing above the wall.

There are the beehives ranged in the sun;
  And down by the brink
Of the brook are her poor flowers, weed-o'rrun,
  Pansy and daffodil, rose and pink.

A year has gone, as the tortoise goes,
  Heavy and slow;
And the same rose blows, and the same sun glows,
  And the same brook sings of a year ago.
    (*AP*, p. 46)

There are shades of Thomas Hood's nostalgic reverie here, and the numerous nineteenth-century editions of Whittier's poetical works which now line the shelves of second-hand bookshops, testify to the popularity of his poetry in England.

Whitman's originality was eventually to be followed by a concerted effort on the part of American poets to break free from the legacy of English literature. T.S. Eliot and Ezra Pound (1885–1972) cultivated an 'international' approach to poetry which rendered the Americanness of Whitman something of an embarrassment, given his undoubted importance. Pound's somewhat grudging recognition of the importance of Whitman is the subject of his brief but revealing poem, *A Pact* (see *PBAV*, p. 280).

By way of contrast, William Carlos Williams (1883–1962), though a friend and admirer of Pound, consciously sought to capture the atmosphere of American urban life in his poetry, which freely adopts American linguistic idioms. His major work was the long poem *Patterson* (1946–58), but in the following extract from *Spring and All* we can appreciate the use to which he puts free verse:

Now the grass, tomorrow
the stiff curl of wildcarrot leaf

One by one objects are defined –
It quickens: clarity, outline of leaf

But now the stark dignity of
entrance – Still, the profound change
has come upon them: rooted they
grip down and begin to awaken
          (*PBAV*, p. 263, ll.20–7)

The whole poem reads like a series of disconnected statements, behind which we can nevertheless discern a potentially logical grammatical sequence. The fragmentary images are vividly realized, it is the overall picture we are continually searching for, and never quite seeing. From the way the poem is written down, Williams's strategy seems to be to defamiliarize the image of an otherwise predictable spring landscape by dismembering it into a random series of word groups. The effect is chaotic and ill-defined; but of course that is what Williams wants us to experience as spring. The new life has as yet no self-consciousness: 'They enter the new world naked,/cold, uncertain of all/save that they enter . . .' (ll.16–18). Clarification, definition and outline only begin to happen once spring has arrived, 'But now the stark dignity of/entrance . . .'.

It was the freshness and originality of men like Williams and Wallace Stevens (1879–1955), Robert Frost (1874–1963), E.E. Cummings (1894–1962) and Robert Lowell (1917–77) that helped to bring about a concerted effort on this side of the Atlantic to introduce free and experimental verse into the somewhat conservative atmosphere of English poetry.

Despite the fact that free verse may take on a range of very different appearances on the page, there lie behind it certain theoretical and technical concepts that can be usefully considered before looking in more detail at specific examples.

Free verse retains the line, the visual sign of 'poetry' on the page; but all formal control of that line is dispensed with save the poet's own instinct for phrasing, coupled with the unit of sense. This can be illustrated briefly here by recalling the regularity of Coleridge's *The Ancient Mariner* ballad verses (though in that poem he did occasionally lengthen his stanzas to a five- and six-line variant). Coleridge establishes a metrical unit which controls the entire poem. Compare that with the 'sprung rhythm' of Hopkins's *The Wreck of the Eurydice*, or with Causley's *My Friend Maloney*; in a poetic environment long since familiar with the spirit of freedom encouraged by free verse, Causley in fact reduces the last line of his final verse to one word without destroying the ballad idiom of his poem. It is his most appropriate 'unit of sense' at that point, and he, rather than any formal metrical pattern dictated by his use of the ballad, is the final arbiter. As we saw from Adrian Mitchell's poem quoted in Chapter 1, free verse may be a step towards freeing the poet even from the line. This is the point at which, by definition, poetry is no longer definable by the term 'verse', which signifies a metrical *line*. But poetry, understood as a linguistic method of communication, need not necessarily operate through verse.

In free verse no guide lines are recognized by the poet except those he himself creates as he creates each poem. He may use rhyme, but it will be where and when he chooses; it is there strictly to serve his meaning, never in relation to a regular pattern. Use of metre is viewed in the same light. The meaning of the poem and the poem alone is paramount; no longer is it a statement on behalf of a representative group of people to be identified as such by its common form. Each poem is formally unique, potentially unclassifiable. It follows that free verse is an extraordinarily difficult medium in which to write successfully. We live in a society of complex cultural and social divisions, many of which are potentially antagonistic; the dominance of a single religious ethic has long since been a thing of the past, and we are now being forced to think in terms of comparative religion. Arguably it can be as difficult to live in such a society, to find oneself, as it is to write poetry *for* such a society. Free verse may indeed reflect the lives of many people today, a process of continual experimentation which can easily become a drift into aimlessness and formlessness.

If the social controls we find in the political structures of Elizabethan and early Jacobean England are reflected in a poetry which embraces the cultural forms of classical art, the social state analogous to free verse would seem to imply anarchy. Yet we do not have anarchy; nor would we be correct in assuming that the constant warnings we hear of impending anarchy are necessarily any more urgent than those delivered in the late sixteenth and early seventeenth centuries. There is no reason to suppose that John Donne was any less sincere or 'correct' when he wrote of his own seventeenth century world:

'Tis all in peeces, all cohaerence gone;
All just supply, and all Relation;*

than W.B. Yeats (1865–1935), who wrote in *The Second Coming*, 'Things fall apart; the centre cannot hold'.

Modern poets have undeniably been dispossessed of the central platform upon which their predecessors stood (and continued to stand long after it had been trundled into a shadowy corner). The result has not been the dissipation of poetry under the concealment of a bogus new style called free verse. While many poets have adopted free verse as, paradoxically, a 'form', what we find as we read and experiment with contemporary poetry is something far more complex and interesting. Poets have taken the formal components of poetry, including the cultural, religious and intellectual points of reference associated with them, and through a continued process of linguistic experiment with those components, sought to perpetuate the art of using language as a medium which can go beyond literal meaning.

They have necessarily tended to do this initially in the light of an individual conviction of what is true, rather than a collective one. The goal, allied to the instinctive search of an artist for an audience, has indeed been to move toward some kind of collectively recognizable statement. In a predominantly secular world where God is not so much absent as continually being rediscovered and redefined in terms of collective, impersonal political and economic forces, the task of the poet has tended towards a reversal of that which Milton envisaged for himself when he sought to 'justifie the wayes of God to men'.

Between blank verse and free verse, therefore, lie a whole range of possibilities, most of which (given our civilized horror of anarchy) have dutifully been classified. Most of these will in some shape or form have had an existence in the writing of poetry from the very first.

It is possible here to consider only a very few examples. The first is an extract from a poem in free verse by Charles Tomlinson (born 1927), *The Churchyard Wall*:

* The First Anniversary, ll.213–14.

Stone against stone, they are building back
   Round the steepled bulk, a wall
That enclosed from the neighbouring road
   The silent community of graves. James Bridle,
Jonathan Silk and Adam Bliss, you are well housed   5
   Dead, howsoever you lived – such headstones
Lettered and scrolled, and such a wall
   To repel the wind. The channel, first,
Dug to contain a base in solid earth
   And filled with the weightier fragments. The propped yews   10
Will scarcely outlast it; for, breached,
   It may be rebuilt. The graves weather
And the stone skulls, more ruinous
   Than art had made them, fade by their broken scrolls.
It protects the dead. The living regard it   15
   Once it is falling, and for the rest
Accept it. Again, the ivy
   Will clasp it down, save for the buried base
And that, where the frost has cracked,
   Must be trimmed, reset, and across its course   20
The barrier raised. Now they no longer
   Prepare: they build, judged by the dead.
    (*TNP*, pp. 142–3, ll.1–22)

Although there is no regular rhyme pattern and no regular metre, Tomlinson does visually imply an ordering of his poetry by his decision to indent alternate lines. But the fact remains that without any obvious formal guide, we are left to rely largely upon our own sensitivity, our own commitment in reading, to discover the full extent of what the poet is saying. We can never be *sure* that we know why the first line stops with 'back' and the second begins with 'Round'. With the loss of publicly accepted rules we are forced into speculations which require us to read with a positive frame of mind, but equally to read with real attention to every aspect of the poet's manipulation of words and phrases.

The subject of the poem is clear from its title, so how does Tomlinson present the wall to us? Solidity is surely the overriding impression of the first two lines. The words that naturally have a heavily stressed quality are spread fairly evenly across the lines, giving a necessarily ponderous effect to the reading. It might be scanned thus:

Stóne against stóne, they are búilding báck
   Roúnd the stéepled búlk, a wáll

The four main stresses in each line encourage a sense of firmness and regularity. That regularity is underpinned by the matching of consonant sounds in line one: 'S*t*one', '*st*one'; '*b*uilding *b*ack'. The alliterative 'b' is picked up in line two with 'bulk', an interesting word to help describe a church, focusing our attention on an attitude of mind rather than a specific image of the building. Finally we note that the subject of the sentence, 'wall', is placed where it will receive the full benefit of its natural stress.

The second half of this sentence flows far more smoothly, and the contrast is important. The words encourage us to slide them together as we read ('elision'), and the natural rhythm would suggest only three stresses: 'That enclósed from the neíghbouring róad'. Aided by consonants the vowel sounds run more easily into each other than in the previous lines: 'Tha*t en*closed' (The final 't' of 'that' and the 'en' of 'enclosed' form a natural link, '— ten —'). In 'Stone against stone' we had the juxtaposition of sounds which required us to pause to make the words clear: 'again*st st*one'. Try to make one 'st' do for both words; it is obviously wrong. The ease with which the third line moves is aided rhythmically by the use of the 'anapest', where each foot is ˘ ˘ ′ .

The point here is that there are two worlds to be considered, separated by the churchyard wall, now being rebuilt: the world of the living, and the world of the dead. The opening lines have indicated that we should be ready for a poem that will be looking to explore this contrast:

                . . . you are well housed
        Dead, howsoever you lived
        (ll.5–6)

'Well housed' denotes a satisfactory state, unchallenged within the line. The impact on this of 'Dead', with its following comma, assuring a pause, is achieved because it comes at the beginning of a new line. It is not openly ironic about the fact that James Bridle, Jonathan Silk and Adam Bliss probably had to wait to die to be 'well housed', but it invites us to reflect on that possibility. The names, of course, are clearly chosen to suggest an earlier generation, and Bridle, Silk and Bliss have evident symbolic implications.

A very practical consideration of the business of building a wall between the living and the dead is next described:

                . . . The channel, first,
        Dúg to contáin a báse in sólid eárth
            And filled with weightier fragments. The propped yews
        Will scarcely outlast it
            (ll.8–11)

The practicality of this description – the language is very plain here – denotes an important aspect of Tomlinson's technique. Free verse gives him the chance to write very simply if he wishes: 'a base in solid earth'. Line nine reads like prose, it does not fall into a rhythmic pattern in the way that line three did, inviting an anapest metre. There are stresses in line nine, but the denial of an inappropriately regular scansion for the whole line is achieved by shifting after 'contain' from an implied anapest to iambic rhythm; the effect is to avoid the dominance of either one.

The wall, as it is gradually rebuilt in the course of the poem (physically around the graves, and also as a concept of partition between life and death), has an unartistic, prosaic quality. It challenges 'poetry', where poetry is the product of contrived (and therefore potentially dishonest) art.

In the extract quoted here, this unpoetic construction comes to challenge one of the favourite symbols of grave-yard poets, the yew tree. Notice again how the subject, 'The propped yews', is stated in one line, giving us the time in the gap between lines to make our own associations with the image; the poet then delivers his judgment in the next line, a challenge to orthodox assumptions. We have already met this technique in 'you are well housed/Dead'. The yews may be propped, but the wall has a superior quality: 'for, breached,/It may be rebuilt.' (ll. 11–12) Again, the line distinction marks a fresh insight, a growth of meaning within the poem. 'Breached' tells of weakness, 'It may be rebuilt' corrects a false impression of vulnerability.

That which is apparently unartistic (including 'unpoetic' free verse, even) has a strength superior to the self-consciously artistic ornamentation of death:

>. . . The graves weather
>And the stone skulls, more ruinous
>Than art had made them, fade by their broken scrolls.
>(ll. 12–14)

In the remaining lines of this extract, note how Tomlinson continues to juxtapose the 'dead' and the 'living' (l. 15). He clearly wants us to reflect on how we come to terms with death, on how we live with it. Our sensitivity towards this issue, and our understanding of his insight into it, is best awakened by his specialized use of language to construct an honest response to the problem, even as the wall, though a construction – a form of 'specialization' in building – is honest, with 'a base in solid earth', and more natural than decorated gravestones. It is not the memorials in the graveyard, a futile attempt to keep us in touch with 'The silent community' of the dead, that enable us to cope; it is our ability to create a barrier between us and them. Later in the poem we read of the builders:

They work at ease, the shade drawn in
To the uncoped wall which casts it, unmindful
  For the moment, that they will be outlasted
By what they create, that their labour
  Must be undone.
     (ll. 26–30)

Tomlinson, a poet influenced by the work of the French symbolists and contemporary American poets (notably William Carlos Williams), is working outward from a personal response to the issue of death, towards a statement that asks us to re-examine attitudes influenced by a religious tradition habitually expressed in traditional artistic, poetic forms. With the declining influence of that religious orthodoxy the formal predictability of its means of expression is also in decline, in concert with the mouldering gravestones and the vulnerable yew trees.

From what it has been possible to say here of the structure of *The Churchyard Wall*, free verse is clearly a stylistic development well suited to the expression of positive alternative views, it does not necessarily mark the onset of incoherence with the passing of traditional social controls. The poem ends with a suggestion of hope in the face of death, but a hope that implies a radical break with orthodox notions of resurrection. The wall symbolizes the existence of a human quality of patience we may all rely on while we wait, longer than perhaps we expect, for the mystery of death to be explained:

. . . They leave completed
Their intent and useful labours to be ignored,
To pass into common life, a particle
  Of the unacknowledged sustenance of the eye,
Less serviceable than a house, but in a world of houses
  A merciful structure. The wall awaits decay.
     (ll. 35–40)

Behind Charles Tomlinson's poem lies the tradition of reflective, philosophical poetry. A continuous monologue where an uninterrupted flow of verse is most suitable.

In the next example, the poet has chosen to use a regular verse pattern, though rhyme and metre are free:

Hawk Roosting

I sit in the top of the wood, my eyes closed.
Inaction, no falsifying dream
Between my hooked head and hooked feet:
Or in sleep rehearse perfect kills and eat.

The convenience of the high trees!   5
The air's buoyancy and the sun's ray
Are of advantage to me;
And the earth's face upward for my inspection.

My feet are locked upon the rough bark.
It took the whole of Creation   10
To produce my foot, my each feather:
Now I hold Creation in my foot

Or fly up, and revolve it all slowly –
I kill where I please because it is all mine.
There is no sophistry in my body: 15
My manners are tearing off heads –

The allotment of death.
For the one path of my flight is direct
Through the bones of the living.
No arguments assert my right: 20

The sun is behind me.
Nothing has changed since I began.
My eye has permitted no change.
I am going to keep things like this.
    (*TNP*, p. 179)

The poet is Ted Hughes (born 1930), a writer fascinated by the poetry of the Middle English period. The directness and under-lying quality of brutality in much of his work seems to reflect the earthiness of such poetry.

It is not difficult to see how Hughes is making use of his verse structure; each set of four lines introduces us to a new facet of his subject. Immediacy is achieved at the outset by his use of the first person. As we read each verse we should look for the stresses created by the phrasing; there is little if any underlying sense of the overall rhythmic pattern we find in Causley, whose verses are frequently composed with the tradition of ballad writing in mind. The more we read this poem, the more it becomes apparent that two heavy stresses at the end of a line help to point up the sense, and as we investigate that possibility, the more we become aware of his use of the word 'my': 'my eýes clósed', 'mý inspéction', 'my eách feáther', 'my fóot', 'my bódy', '. . . it is all míne'. The emphasis is especially clear with the phrase '*my* each feather', because grammatically the word is unnecessary.

As Tomlinson was evidently writing about much more than a wall, so Hughes is certainly writing much more than a poem which imagines what it would be like if a hawk could speak. This is, at a deeper level, a poem about megalomania; the hawk proudly sees everything about him as inferior creation put there to serve him:

The convénience of the hígh trées!
The aír's búoyancy and the sún's ray
Are of advántage to me;
And the eárth's fáce upward for my inspéction.

The last line reveals a somewhat partial (not to say eccentric) way of perceiving the reason why the surface of the earth faces upward! There must equally be a note of irony here for a readership bombarded with conservationist arguments. The hawk is in no position to declare 'I am going to keep things like this' (l.24). But then, are we putting ourselves in the hawk's place in order to disagree? If so, are we as humans any more justified in the confidence *we* have in our vision of our own mastery of creation?

The chief quality the poet represents the hawk possessing is a single-minded practicality. All feeling, all emotion, is weakness. Human beings are by implication charged with sentimentality; 'high trees' are attractive to the hawk only in so far as they are 'convenient' (l.5). There is 'no falsifying dream/between my hooked head and hooked feet', 'There is no sophistry in my body', 'No arguments assert my right'. It is all so brutally simple and functional, and for me it is disturbing to find that Hughes would seem to be commending the hawk's violent 'energy' to his human readers (see *BP*, pp. 389–90).

The debate generated by this poem is complex, and through the poetry it is made all the more real and urgent. Rhyme, on the one occasion in the first verse where it is used, and alliteration emphasize and sharpen the images of brutality, as do the four blunt sentences into which the final verse is divided; there is an implicit denial here of any need for an 'argument' to be carried forward from line to line and verse to verse. Civilization, with its polite, discursive respectability – resting largely on its perfection of polite, discursive language – is revealed as a mask, and the poet who now lives in a world that has tumbled out of that comfortable bed is left to find a form of words that will not lie: 'My manners are tearing off heads'. I feel bound to suggest that other alternatives could be found!

Both *The Churchyard Wall* and *Hawk Roosting* are poems which respond to fundamental questions by no means best understood as specifically 'modern'. Yet in form and content both poems reflect the poets' dissatisfaction with the way those issues have previously been considered. Religious orthodoxy is questioned by Tomlinson, while Hughes reassesses the point of reference which became central for so many poets as the eighteenth century progressd, the natural world. Hughes is often described as a 'nature poet', but it is important in this respect to compare *Hawk Roosting* with, for example, the passage from Wordsworth's *Prelude* already quoted in the previous chapter.

For Wordsworth, nature served ultimately as a source of revelation for the existence of a benign deity. In his early work God and Nature become virtually synonymous. Where nature cannot be represented as soothing and reassuring, its sublimity will point beyond to a just God; where harshness and contradiction appear, they are always resolvable, ultimately concordant. Wordsworth's contemplation of natural objects made it possible for him to perceive:

That what we feel of sorrow and despair
From ruin and from change, and all the grief
That passing shows of Being leave behind,
Appeared an idle dream, that could maintain,
Nowhere, dominion o'er the enlightened spirit
Whose meditative sympathies repose
Upon the breast of Faith
(*The Excursion*, Book I, ll.949–55, *WPW*, p. 602)

In this specific instance the poet has called to mind 'Those weeds, and the high spear-grass on that wall,/By mist and silent rain drops silvered o'er', an 'image of tranquility' (ll.943–6).

While this is very much in keeping with the philosophical climate of Wordsworth's time, Hughes is patently a product of the twentieth century, his poetry challenging Romantic concepts of nature and their significance.

Modern poetry is by no means only the product of a sense of dislocation with the past. This becomes evident when we consider various 'schools' of poetry that have emerged as the century has progressed. These often constitute only loosely knit groups of poets, united sometimes by their opposition to the philosophy and methods of other contemporary groups, as well as in their sense of what should constitute the priorities of their art.

Two such influential groupings which came into being in the mid 1950s were the Movement (influenced particularly by Philip Larkin), and the Group (founded by Philip Hobsbaum). At its inception, the Movement represented a reaction against what it saw as contemporary trends in English poetry away from its native traditions of rhyme and scansion towards free verse, and an inflated emotionalism. A.A. Alvarez, himself an influential poet and critic, responded scornfully to the philosophy of Movement poets in his introduction to *The New Poetry* (1962), an anthology he edited for Penguin Books:

Sometime in the twenties Thomas Hardy remarked to Robert Graves that '*vers libre* could come to nothing in England. "All we can do is to write on the old themes in the old styles, but try to do a little better than those who went before us."' Since about 1930 the machinery of modern English poetry seems to have been controlled by a series of negative feed-backs designed to produce precisely the effect Hardy wanted.
(*TNP*, p. 21)

Long before this Larkin had emphasized the important influence on his own work of Hardy's poetry (see *BP*, p. 127).

So marked could the 'feed-back' effect of Movement theory be that the work of one of its adherants in the 1950s, Donald Davie, has been described as 'neo-Augustan', implying a return to something analogous to the effect created by the ordered couplets of Goldsmith, if not Pope or Dryden (see, for example, *Green River* in *BP*, p. 134). It is worth noting that Davie's poetry has changed considerably in recent years, a warning to us that categorization may misrepresent the poet as often as it may help to reveal him.

Poets who became associated with the Group (they include Peter Porter, Peter Redgrove and George Macbeth) evinced a far more liberal attitude towards style; but, as with Movement poets, the unifying factor was a sense of the need to redefine and thus reaffirm the poet's role in the context of protest. Edward Lucie-Smith, who took over Hobsbaum's role as chairman for the regular seminars held by Group poets, describes them thus:

Essentially, what one finds in their work is the note of radical protest which one also finds in the dramatists who established themselves in the fifties, such as Osborne and Wesker. They are looser, more colloquial, more deliberately naturalistic than most of the poets of the Movement.
(*BP*, p. 179)

An overall picture begins to emerge, with Group poets, Movement poets, Alvarez's New Poetry, post-Movement poets, a school of Scottish poets, and a number of other overlapping formulations, of an active, not to say frenetic world of British poetry, very much alive to and often influenced by contemporary American writing, and, less markedly, contemporary European poetry. Behind all this creativity and critical appraisal lies a peculiarly contemporary concern, one I have emphasized in previous chapters, and here referred to by Alvarez commenting on the Movement:

. . . with their deliberate common sense and understatement, some of the Movement poets command, at their best, a self-contained strength and a concern for the discipline of verse which is vital if the art is to remain public. The question is the kind of success a style allows.
(*TNP*, p. 29)

A style which, because of its basis in a specific cultural context, may be felt by the poet to compromise his or her convictions, can be abandoned; but as the myriad groupings show only too clearly, poets work within a social context, even if it is a fragmented one, and some degree of alignment is inevitable. As often as not, the search for a poetic voice that will 'remain public' has led poets to adapt and modify existing styles. In the case of the following poem by Philip Hobsbaum, we find him utilizing the basic structure of the iambic pentameter, and attempting to steer a course mid-way between the traditional demands of blank verse for an inflated rhetoric, and the no less stringent rhyming discipline of the couplet, by using 'half' or 'imperfect' rhyme. His meaning requires him to convey a sense of control to his reader, but control without rigidity. His poem is concerned with personal circumstances where a socially acceptable marriage relationship is being preserved, but only precariously:

A Secret Sharer

'Tell me of the house where you were born
Near Tandragee – the field, the chicken-run,
The single shop more than a mile away,
The village even farther. Make me see
You waiting while your idiot neighbour pumps,   5
Your youth a murmur under Tilly lamps.
Did you walk out under the clear cold stars
To where the lights of Lisburn blur the skies
Or sit over the peat fire's acrid blaze,
Hair falling carelessly about your face   10

And think of me, or someone not unlike?'
The picture fades into the usual dark
That keeps us separate. You have your past,
I mine, trampled to city soot and dust –
So smile, and shake your head. Our lives were such,   15
Spent years apart, that thoughts can barely touch,
But bodies do much better. At a nod,
Without a word we slide into your bed
To clutch in a shared spasm. Once apart
I rise, rub myself down, bid you good night: 20
We shared a room, a bed, but not a life.
And so I leave and go home to my wife,
Whiling away in speech the hours that wane
Until my body talks to yours again.
    (*BP*, pp. 181–2)

   Half rhyme denotes only a partial compatability of sounds, as
in 'born/run' (ll.1–2), 'pumps/lamps' (ll.5–6) and 'blaze/face'
(ll.9–10); it is thus a fitting technical framework for a poem concerned with divisive antagonisms that exist within the poet's own
life. The incompleteness of his fragmented personality is illustrated primarily through the account he gives of his relationship
with his mistress. The poet is a sophisticated product of the city (a
writer of poetry, no less!), the girl is of Irish peasant stock, and so
vast is the social and cultural gap between them, that verbal
communication is impossible. There is consequently a disjunction
within the poet of physical love, and the 'official' state of a marriage partnership, where, ironically, he can 'while away' his time
'in speech', 'Until my body talks to yours again' (ll.23–4).
   We should note an interesting lapse on the part of Hobsbaum
into the poetic rhetoric of blank verse. While his lines are primarily colloquial in their phraseology, in particular the very effective 'And so I leave and go home to my wife' (l.22), where the
natural tendency to give equally strong stresses to 'go home'
breaks up the regularity of the iambic pentameter, line six, 'Your
youth a murmur under Tilly lamps' strikes a very different note.
The imaginative linking of the abstract concept of 'youth' with
the concrete immediacy of 'murmur' is poetic in its suggestive-
ness, but out of keeping with the rest of the poem. We should
consider whether it is misjudged, or whether the poem gains anything from it.
   One final point to make is that, as a twentieth-century love
poem, *A Secret Sharer* provides us with an interesting comparison
to sixteenth-century love poetry. It is the verbalization of love
that Hobsbaum's subject cannot share with his mistress. They

share the physical act of love, but he needs to do more, and to *share* that additional expression of love with the Irish girl. His need will evidently never be gratified, and the poem is thus an expression of isolation, a general comment on social fragmentation and the demise of an 'audience'. The sixteenth-century love poet often wrote despairing professions of love for a socially superior woman, knowing physical consummation to be impossible, but knowing full well that his poetry could and would be read by the object of his desires. The latter was a work effectively confirming the cohesiveness of society, especially as the 'mistress' thus addressed would more often than not be already well married within her class.

Contemporary poets, regardless of their individual allegiances, have all worked from the understanding that they have the freedom to question what issues are appropriate to their art. They need not feel obliged to write within the formal categories of, for example, epic, love poetry, or satire. Technical presentation has become equally a matter for their own personal judgment; an understandably 'democratic' state of affairs for post-Romantic poets. It has therefore seemed logical to some of them to ask whether all such attempts of the kind we have so far considered might not be futile. What use is poetry that has sloughed off outmoded, irrelevant linguistic conventions, if it does no more than use its new language in essentially the same way as the old? If the language may no longer be trusted, neither may the process of reasoning and explanation which it was designed to serve.

Some poets have therefore investigated language, not as a vehicle for connected reasoning, but as a purveyor of sounds. Sentences, phrases and words are broken down into their constituent parts to enable us to re-examine the medium without the impediment of an expressed belief or conviction. Belief and conviction underpinned art in previous centuries, but have been exposed as destructive to those who view single-minded notions of 'the truth' with profound scepticism in the light of two world wars and the rhetorical warfare of capitalism and communism.

Such poetry is arguably achieving an integrity that is unattainable through any other linguistic convention. Its discontinuities at the level of orthodox language use render it all the more 'concrete' at a higher level of linguistic purity. Concrete poetry is one logical outcome of the abandonment of formal grammar in the search for literary purity of expression. This is Edwin Morgan's concrete poem, in which he explores 'Pomander', a ball of perfumes, usually encased in a perforated globe or box. Sound, sense, and indeed shape are of equal significance, though 'sense' here does not mean 'argument' or 'point of view':

                    pomander
                open pomander
              open poem and her
              open poem and him
             open poem and hymn
            hymn and hymen leander
             high man pen meander
             o pen poem me and her
            pen me poem me and him
              om mane padme hum
            pad me home panda hand
           open up o holy panhandler
          ample panda pen or bamboo pond
         ponder a bonny poem pomander opener
        open banned peon penman hum and banter
      open hymn and pompom band and panda hamper
           o i am a pen open man or happener
             i am open manner happener
               happy are we open
                poem and a pom
               poem and a panda
               poem and aplomb

                                                              (*BP*, p. 320)

   After my lengthy theoretical introduction to concrete poetry, it is very important to add that the poetry itself will not always be in a similarly serious vein. *Pomander* works when it is found to be fun, it is a witty blend of word-play and strong rhythmic currents. Concrete poetry can certainly function at a philosophically taxing level, and Morgan's *Opening the Cage* is an example of this (*BP*, p.319); but the philosophy in question is one that directs the art of poetry away from involvement with anything other than poetry itself. *Opening the Cage* is subtitled by the poet as '14 variations on 14 words', the words being a quote from John Cage: 'I have nothing to say and I am saying it and that is poetry'. Morgan himself, incidentally, has written in free verse, and very impressively so:

The domain of Arnheim was all snow, but we were there.
We saw a yellow light thrown on the icefield
from the huts by the pines, and laughter came up

floating from a white corrie
miles away, clearly.
We moved on down, arm in arm.
    (*From the Domain of Arnheim*, ll.4–9, *BP*, p. 317)

Even here, Morgan is attempting to distance himself from the
normal human perspective of the scene, representing the narrator
as one of a company visiting the planet from outer space. They see
Arnheim as it was in prehistoric times, but the visitors have no
earthly time-sense; theirs is a detached perception of the kind
which potentially might enable us to see what is familiar as new,
and to discover a quality of beauty beyond human understanding, though in some mysterious way it may be made tenable
for us through art.

   The Domain of Arnheim is also the title of a short story by
Edgar Allen Poe (1809–49). The story introduces us to a man
called Ellison who has the opportunity – through the happy
combination of his personal artistic genius and access to unlimited
funds – to fulfil his dream of creating the perfect work of art.
'The fullest, if not the sole proper satisfaction of this sentiment he
instinctively felt to lie in the creation of novel forms of beauty.'
This urge is further refined by a belief that 'the sole legitimate
field for the poetic exercise, lies in the creation of novel moods of
purely *physical* loveliness'. Anything which involves 'ethical
speculations' is rejected. Thought of in conjunction with concrete
poetry, we can see how there the speculative or argumentative
content gives way to a far more 'physical' experience of the poem.
For Poe's central character, these considerations lead him to a
pursuit of his artistic ideal through the creation of a landscape
garden.

   What Poe is advocating is the need for art to involve a degree of
what he calls 'strangeness'; it is this quality that will free the mind
of its constricting opinions, assumptions and prejudices,
ennabling it to view the world anew. Poe's Domain is briefly
described as a seductive, exotic dream world; Morgan's twentieth-
century Domain is cold, harsh and primitive. As his extra-
terrestrial travellers make their way through the bleak, prehistoric
landscape, they meet with nothing but fear and aggression.

   Ellison is an isolated poet, with only a few friends who share his
vision. Poe's reference to his creation as 'similar in kind, although
infinitely superior, to that which so long distinguished Fonthill',
invites us to compare him with William Beckford, the
misanthropic eighteenth-century recluse who built Fonthill
Abbey in mock Gothic style. If the poet is to assume an alien-like

position (and Beckford certainly did), it is only to be expected that his potential readers may be inclined to respond in the aggressive manner of Morgan's stone-age inhabitants of Arnheim. Morgan implies that this is a sad but unredeemable situation: '. . . we had no power/over their fear. If one of them had been dying/he would have died.' Poe's Ellison seems well satisfied with the élitist privacy which surrounds his poetic vision. Many contemporary poets, however, are actively concerned by their inability to reach wider audiences than they do.

In 1963 John Wain wrote despairingly that 'the mass middle-brow public distrusts and fears poetry' (*BP* p. 387), and one image of the modern poet is of a being not wholly unlike Coleridge's wild-eyed Ancient Mariner, desperately seeking an audience from amongst an indifferent crowd, and having found it, striving to keep it. What has become clear is that the problem of finding a readership cannot be solved by putting the clock back. Something of that awareness is present in Wain's poem, *The New Sun*:

The new sun rises in the year's elevation,
over the low roofs' perspective.

It reveals the roughness of winter skin
and the dinginess of winter clothes.

It draws, with a hard forefinger,
a line under the old ways.

Finis! the old ways have become obsolete,
the old skin, the old clothes.
    (*TNP*, p. 125, ll.1–8)

Poets have to recognize the circumstances of their cultural environment as the basis from which they make their statements, regardless of their admiration for poetry of the previous centuries.
    The study of modern poetry – through individuals and the manifestos of various groups – reveals at least one concern which has assumed the status of a widely held conviction: poetry must, in some way, seek to place itself within the collective experience of the society for which it is written. What was once a part of the collective experience of the literate in Shakespeare's or Milton's time is not now readily available to us, and without some notion of what that might have been we will be unable to establish the positive, creative relationship with the text necessary for a reading of poetry. Words on the page can always mean something to us,

but poetry is an exacting art, and always demands more than a vague sense of meaning. The experience of being left cold by a poem, be it ancient or modern, will not occur as a result of a failure to understand the technicalities of the piece, it will be the consequence of the absence of a sense of mutual concern. In the case of poetry written in the past, especially pre-Romantic poetry, this means that we do have to be prepared to study context. If we are ready to do that, we will soon discover that the other side of the same coin will reveal an often startling degree of continuing relevance.

Coming to terms with the distance which has opened up between ourselves and the collective experience of those who lived two or three centuries ago is not to suggest, as Arnold seems to have concluded, that there is now no collective experience left; it is simply to say that it has changed, as it has always been changing.

This point has been wittily made by the Scottish poet Hugh MacDiarmid (1892–1978). *Glasgow 1960* is a plea for poets to recognize how times have changed. His vision, that of a massive crowd flocking to hear a philosophical debate as they would to see Celtic play Rangers, and of the popular press headlining a new book of abstruse verse by a Turkish poet, is an ironic description of a situation which subconsciously most poets still probably long for, but which is here satirically exposed as totally unrealistic:

Returning to Glasgow after long exile
Nothing seemed to me to have changed its style.
Buses and trams labelled 'To Ibrox'
Swung past packed tight as they'd hold with folks.
Football match, I concluded, but just to make sure
I asked; and the man looked at me fell dour,
Then said, 'Where in God's name are *you* frae, sir?
It'll be a record gate, but the cause o' the stir
Is a debate on "la loi de l'effort converti"
Between Professor MacFadyen and a Spanish pairty.
I gasped. The newsboys came running along,
'Special! Turkish Poet's Abstruse New Song.
Scottish Authors' Opinions' — and, holy snakes,
I saw the edition sell like hot cakes.
    (*BP*, p. 45)

SUGGESTIONS FOR FURTHER READING

The following books concern themselves with poetry in specific periods: Janet Coleman, *Medieval Readers and Writers 1350–1400* (London, Hutchinson, 1981); Murray Roston, *Sixteenth-Century English Literature* (London, Macmillan, 1982); a more specialized treatment, challenging a number of ideas accepted by Roston, is John N. King, *English Reformation Literature* (Princeton, NJ, Princeton UP, 1982); James Turner, *The Politics of Landscape: Rural Scenery and Society in English Poetry 1630–1660* (Oxford, Basil Blackwell, 1979). In the following book Raymond Williams discusses poetry and prose (his account of late Augustan and Romantic poetry is particularly helpful): *The Country and the City* (London, Chatto and Windus, 1973); W.A. Speck, *Society and Literature in England 1700–60* (Dublin, Gill and Macmillan, 1983); Isobel Armstrong, *Language as Living Form in Nineteenth Century Poetry* (Brighton, Harvester, 1982); M.L. Rosenthal, *The New Poets* (London, OUP, 1967); J.M. Cohen, *Poetry of This Age 1908–1965* (London, Hutchinson, 1966); my personal preference has always been for interesting anthologies of modern verse, rather than extended critical works; one such not referred to in this book is *Poetry 1900–1975* ed. George MacBeth (London, Longman, 1983).

Two books which take a far broader view are: Denys Thompson, *The Uses of Poetry* (Cambridge, CUP, 1978); and Anthony Easthope, *Poetry as Discourse* (London, Methuen, 1983). Thompson discusses the need met by poetry and the purposes proposed for it, reaching back as far as it is historically possible to go. Easthope's range is from Shakespeare to Eliot, and he uses a good deal of interesting technical analysis in his discussion. His approach provides an interesting contrast to Denys Thompson.

An important recent study of poet/reader relationships is David Trotter, *The Making of the Reader* (London, Macmillan, 1984). Trotter writes about the changes which have occurred since Wordsworth's time, and finishes with an interesting section on the teaching of poetry in schools. A standard survey of readership is Richard D. Altick, *The English Common Reader* (Chicago, University of Chicago Press, 1963).

Unlike the texts so far mentioned, the following are not based on a traditionally chronological approach. A sense of context remains (more centrally for some than others), but it is the intention of these texts to discuss poetry through a more concentratedly theoretical approach: E.L. Epstein, *Language and Style* (London, Methuen, 1978); G.S. Fraser, *Metre, Rhyme and Free Verse* (London, Methuen, 1983); Millar and Currie, *The Language of Poetry* (London, Heineman, 1982); Clive T. Probyn, *English Poetry* (Harlow, Longman, 1984).

Offering a different experience from the previous texts is Geoffrey Grigson, *Private Art: A Poetry Notebook* (London, Allison and Busby, 1981).

The topic of translations was touched on briefly in the second chapter of this book. The debate is by no means restricted to the sixteenth century, and is developed in relation to Dryden, Eliot and Pound in Charles Tomlinson, *Poetry and Metamorphosis* (Cambridge, CUP, 1983).

INDEX